D0592101

Happy Birthday 2013!

from: Cathy

A MAN AFTER GOD'S OWN HEART

DEVOTIONAL

JIM GEORGE

HARVEST HOUSE PUBLISHERS
EUGENE, OREGON

Cover photo © Allioy Photography / Veer

Cover by Garborg Design Works, Savage, Minnesota

A MAN AFTER GOD'S OWN HEART DEVOTIONAL
Copyright © 2012 by Jim George
Published by Harvest House Publishers
Eugene, Oregon 97402
www.harvesthousepublishers.com

ISBN 978-0-7369-4504-2 (pbk.)
ISBN 978-0-7369-4505-9 (eBook)

Printed in China

12 13 14 15 16 17 18 19 20 / FC-NI / 10 9 8 7 6 5 4 3 2 1

A Note
from Jim

In my earlier books *A Man After God's Own Heart* and *A Husband After God's Own Heart,* I pointed to Acts 13:22 to explain what it means to follow after God's heart. God states, "I have found David the son of Jesse, a man after My own heart, who will do all My will." Now, David wasn't perfect. In fact, he was far from perfect! But God saw something in his heart. God saw a man who had a heart that, when confronted by God, desired to correct his ways and get back on track with Him. Though David was less than ideal, he was still fully committed to progressing in his desire to follow God.

It is my prayer that this practical book of exhortations and inspirational thoughts will help you remember that God is not looking for perfection. All He asks for is a man who is progressing in his desire to become a man after God's own heart.

Jim George

Taking Your Decisions to God

Every major accomplishment in a man's life requires a high level of commitment. I'm sure you can remember such an accomplishment in your life. Perhaps you were starting your own business. Or you were considering a job change or mapping out a new direction for your company or family. Whatever it was, you probably felt some initial hesitancy. One day you were eager to start…and the next you weren't so sure. But once you made the decision to proceed, all the long hours of effort were worth it because of the joy of seeing the fruit of your labors.

What major decision or change are you facing right now? Have you included God in the planning process? Take time to pray and share your thoughts and concerns with Him, and ask for His leading as you move forward.

God, I commit my plans to You today. Help me to honor You in all I do. Thank You for guiding me so that my decisions will glorify You and bless the people around me. Amen.

The Price of Commitment

King David understood the necessity of pouring himself fully into his commitments. When it came time to obtain land so he could build an altar to God, someone offered to give David some land for free. But David knew that the greater the commitment, the greater would be the blessing. Therefore he declared he would not offer burnt offerings to God "with that which costs me nothing" (2 Samuel 24:24).

David declined what was convenient, and expressed his love and commitment to God through personal sacrifice. In what ways have you recently expressed your level of commitment to the Lord? Have there been costs involved? You will reap blessings as you wholeheartedly follow God and do what He says. Consider what God said about David: "I have found [him]…a man after My own heart, who will do all My will" (Acts 13:22).

> God, strengthen me so that when my commitment is put to the test, I won't falter. Help me to be a man of my word in my relationships with others and with You. Amen.

God Looks at the Heart

When God sent the prophet Samuel to look for a new king for Israel, He cautioned him, "The LORD does not see as man sees; for man looks at the outward appearance, but the LORD looks at the heart" (1 Samuel 16:7). In everything, God looks on the heart. Your relationship with Him has to do with your heart and your heart's desire. As happened with King David, you may experience lapses in your walk with God. We all do! But whenever that happened, David always returned to God in obedience. That's what made him a man after God's own heart.

Does that describe you as well? No matter what happens, is the deepest desire of your heart to yield yourself fully to Him in obedience? If yes, you'll become a man God can—and will—use.

God, I'm amazed that You don't give up on me when I fail. I do want to walk in obedience, to be free from sin, and to see You move in and through my life. Amen.

What God Desires in You

David was a man with feet of clay, a man who committed sins that grieved God's heart. Yet over the long haul, he sought to be righteous, and his desire was to do God's will. This is the kind of man God looks for. David wasn't perfect, and he didn't deserve God's blessings. But in his heart he had the right desire—a longing to follow and please God.

Is that your personal longing as well? You may feel that being a man after God's heart is too lofty a goal because of some of your past actions. But remember: God looked at David's *heart*. And that's where He's going to look in your life as well. When it comes to becoming a man after God's heart, you can count on God's grace—a grace that enables and strengthens you at all times.

God, You know my heart better than I do. Help me to open my heart to You every day. Purify my heart, I pray, and renew me from the inside out. Amen.

Seek First
His Kingdom

We hear a lot of talk about establishing priorities in our lives. But no one said it better than Jesus: "Do not worry, saying, 'What shall we eat?' or 'What shall we drink?' or 'What shall we wear?'...But seek first the kingdom of God and His righteousness, and all these things shall be added to you" (Matthew 6:31,33). Food, drink, and clothing are important, but they're not your first priority. Rather, your pursuit of God—and the resulting spiritual growth—is what really matters. When you put God first, He will provide for you and your family. That's His promise—seek Him, and He will take care of everything else. As C.S. Lewis said, "Put first things first and we get second things thrown in: put second things first and we lose both first and second things."

Jesus, thank You for inviting me to seek Your kingdom. You are more than just my first priority—all my priorities find their rightful place in You and Your kingdom. Amen.

Yielding to God

When God looks at your life, what does He look for? Not perfection—being a Christian doesn't mean you don't sin anymore. Rather, it means sin is no longer the predominant pattern of your life. As a Christian, you are a new creature in Christ (2 Corinthians 5:17). And when you do sin, because the Holy Spirit lives in you, you are convicted and possess a desire to repent so the joy of your fellowship with God can be restored (Psalm 51:12).

God never asks you to do something without providing you with the enablement to do it. With the Holy Spirit's help, you can live as a man after God's own heart. As you yield your life fully to the Lord, the Spirit will produce fruit that is consistent with being a child of God.

Lord, You can do anything—even make me a man after Your own heart. Thank You for forgiving me and for continuing to make me the man You want me to be. Amen.

Planted in God's Word

Just as water is the only thing that can relieve thirst in the desert, God's Word is the only thing that can satisfy our spiritual thirst. It alone can nourish us spiritually and help us grow as Christians.

So if you want to live as a man after God's own heart, you need to make sure you're firmly planted in God's Word. God has much to say about life and your priorities, and if you neglect the Bible, you will find yourself spiritually malnourished and drifting without direction in life.

If you want to live as a man after God's own heart, then there's no better place for you to go for guidance. Don't you agree? What impact is the Bible having on your life right now? What would making the Bible your first priority involve?

Father, thank You for the Bible! Help me to never take for granted the opportunity to let Your Word shape my thinking, my speaking, and my actions. Amen.

The Keys to Your Growth

When it comes to spiritual growth, God doesn't leave you on your own. His Spirit, who lives in every believer, gives you the power and desire to grow. He is your Guide and Helper (John 14:16-17,26).

Between the Bible and the Holy Spirit, you have everything you need to grow spiritually. And the more you grow, the more God can use you. He can work through you to touch the lives of others—your wife, your children, your co-workers, your fellow churchgoers, your friends and neighbors.

Ultimately, if you want your life to count, you need to grow spiritually. And because Scripture offers everything you need for nourishment, it needs to remain top priority in your life. The more you crave God's Word, the more you'll grow and have an impact.

Lord, thank You for giving me everything I need to continue growing more and more like You. Help me to never give up, never settle for less, and always rely on Your Word. Amen.

Making a Difference in Others

What's remarkable about spiritual growth is the way it can impact every area of your life. As you grow, you please God and become mature as a Christian, and you also see a positive effect on your relationships with others. Each of us, as Christian men, husbands, fathers, and workers, have contact with many people—people whose lives we can impact if we're growing spiritually.

If you want to be a strong, maturing man of God, your first priority is to develop a closer relationship with God. That means spending time with Him in prayer and in His Word. As you seek His guidance and wisdom, You'll give Him the opportunity to work through you so as to point others to Him. There's no better way to make your life count for all eternity.

> *God, I'm amazed that You could use me to make a difference in other people's lives! Renew my heart and mind, I pray, and let Your life in me spill out onto everyone I meet. Amen.*

Hungering After God's Word

John Wesley was greatly devoted to reading the Bible. He laid hold of the Bible because his heart's desire was to grow…and the Bible laid hold of him as well. Every year, he lifted up this prayer as a covenant to God, expressing his desire to grow:

> O blessed Jesus…You have been pleased to give me your holy laws as the Rule of my life…subscribing to all your laws as holy, just, and good, I solemnly take them as the Rule of my words, thoughts, and actions; promising that…I will endeavor to order and govern my whole life according to your direction…

When you commit yourself to growing spiritually and following God's Word, then God, by His grace, will enable you to fulfill all the responsibilities He has given you. Through His power, you'll accomplish great things for Him.

> *Lord, I confess that I can't fulfill Your vision for my life in my own strength. May Your Word and Your Spirit guide me today and empower me to do everything You've called me to do. Amen.*

Staying Faithful

Spiritual growth is a lifelong pursuit. You grow in spiritual maturity moment by moment, day by day, year by year. It doesn't happen instantly—it is a steady but sure process that takes place over time and requires ongoing attention.

In many ways, spiritual exercise is a lot like physical exercise. When you stop exercising physically, your body might not show the results of inactivity for a while. But one day you'll wake up and find everything is sagging in the wrong places.

The same goes for your spiritual life. As you gradually neglect prayer and time in God's Word, at first you might not notice the effects. But they'll catch up to you eventually, and you'll find your spiritual productivity sagging. That's why it's so vital to remain steadfast even in the little things of the Christian life.

Lord, being faithful in prayer and Bible reading day after day is sometimes difficult for me. Open my eyes so I can see the changes You want to make in my life and the progress we're making. Amen.

Keeping the Right Balance

It's not hard for us to stir up the motivation to do the things we *want* to do, is it? While we may find it hard to get excited about making repairs around the house or going to work in the morning, we are usually energetic and enthused when it comes to enjoying a personal hobby or taking time for recreation.

The activities that motivate you—whether it be sports, fishing, hiking, swimming, or whatever—can be either positive or negative. There's nothing wrong with having fun. The key is making sure you don't neglect your priorities when you pursue your interests.

For example, is your spiritual life suffering on account of personal pleasures? Your family life? Being a man after God's own heart means evaluating your choices and keeping the right balance between priorities and time for self.

> *Father, all I have is Yours. Help me to keep my priorities straight so I can be a good steward of the time and energy You have given me. Amen.*

First Things First

Every single day, you'll find yourself repeatedly having to make the choice between priorities and personal pursuits. Ultimately your decision will come down to this: Have I put God and His Word first? Have I taken care of my God-given responsibilities, or neglected them?

You'll find it helpful to invite the Lord to help you with your choices. Make a conscious effort to involve Him in your daily decisions. Take time to pray and communicate your thoughts. Ask Him if there are any biblical principles that might help you make a right decision. As you do all these things, you'll put Proverbs 3:5-6 to work in your life: "Trust in the LORD with all your heart, and lean not on your own understanding; in all your ways acknowledge Him, and He shall direct your paths."

God, teach me how to acknowledge You in everything I do. Whenever I make a decision—big or little, consciously or subconsciously—help me to know the joy of putting You first. Amen.

Freedom from Sin's Effects

Jesus put the seriousness of sin into perspective when He said that even if you merely get angry with someone, you have committed murder in your heart (Matthew 5:22). And even if you lust after a woman in your mind, you have committed adultery with her in your heart (Matthew 5:28).

The bottom line is that any sin, whether big or small, overt or covert, is an affront to God and must be confessed and forsaken. Anytime you have unconfessed sin in your life, it will hurt your relationship with God, stunt your spiritual growth, and affect your loved ones and your work.

When you acknowledge your sin to God, you'll experience the wonderful cleansing that comes with confession: "*Blessed* is he whose transgression is forgiven, whose sin is covered" (Psalm 32:1).

> *Lord, I want to be more like You—free from sin. Show me ways that I've given sin a foothold in my life. Thank You for forgiving and cleansing me! Amen.*

A Lifelong Learner

If you want to grow, it's necessary to be a learner. And God's Word will always be your main source of spiritual nourishment. I once heard a startling statistic that reported less than five percent of all Christians have read through their Bible even once. That means the simple practice of reading the Bible regularly will put you in the top percentile of all believers—and to read the entire Bible in one year takes only about five to ten minutes a day.

Determining to read through your Bible is a decision only you can make. Others can't make it for you. You might find it helpful to follow a Bible-reading schedule. You can also ask someone to help hold you to your commitment. Accountability to a friend will motivate you to follow through on this goal.

God, I want to be a lifelong learner. Help me to build a habit of regularly reading Your Word, and open my eyes and ears so I can take in Your truth. Amen.

Doing Your Part

Over the years I've met with different men who have helped me grow as a Christian. I owe them a tremendous debt! Eventually I grew to the point where I could start meeting with spiritually younger men and sharing with them what I had learned from my mentors.

The Bible strongly encourages men like you and me to get involved in such discipleship. The apostle Paul wrote, "The things you have heard me say in the presence of many witnesses entrust to reliable men who will also be qualified to teach others" (2 Timothy 2:2).

That verse brings to mind a relay race. We're to take the baton of God's truth and pass it on to the next generation of believers. Are you doing your part in the race? Learn from wise Christian men, then pass that wisdom on to others.

> *Lord, help me to find someone on the path just ahead of me who can help me find my way. And help me to find someone just behind me who can learn from my experience. Amen.*

The Blessings of Growth

When it comes to spiritual growth, you can't rest on yesterday's progress. It's like eating food—your need for nourishment is constant, which means getting into your Bible daily and praying regularly.

If you're thinking, *That isn't easy!* you are right. While it's true growing spiritually mature requires action on your part, the benefits are well worthwhile, including…

- greater closeness to God
- spiritual strength for resisting temptation
- wisdom and love you need for guiding your family

The fact we can enjoy these kinds of blessings motivates me, by God's grace, to keep growing mature. I pray that is your desire as well!

Father, when I'm tempted to cut corners or just give up, prompt me by Your Spirit with reminders of the tremendous blessings that come from spending time with You. Amen.

Calling on
the Lord

When you read through the Bible, it becomes clear that men who desire God are men of prayer. For example, Abraham, throughout his life, built altars and called on the name of the Lord. Moses constantly prayed for direction as he led the nation of Israel. Solomon prayed for wisdom so he could judge the nation rightly. Nehemiah prayed for God's protection throughout the rebuilding of Jerusalem's wall. Paul prayed constantly for the churches where he had ministered.

If you've found it a challenge to pray regularly, you're not alone. It's easy to let the things of everyday life crowd out your time for prayer. You can change that by setting aside a specific time each day for meeting with God. Pick a time and stick with it—and you'll enjoy a more vibrant relationship with God.

> *God, help me to establish a realistic and consistent habit of meeting with You in prayer. Thank You for reminding me that great men of God have always made prayer a priority. Amen.*

Mastering the
Art of Prayer

Bible teacher J. Oswald Sanders said the amount of time you give to something indicates its importance to you. With that in mind, would you say there is room for improvement in your prayer life?

If your desire is to live as a man after God's own heart, you'll want to give prayer the time it deserves. In addition to having a set time for prayer each day, you'll want to pray at other times during the day—such as while you're exercising, driving, or waiting in line at the store or bank. If you are alert to such opportunities, you'll be surprised at how often you can lift up your thoughts and concerns to God. The more you take advantage of these times, the more you'll find yourself mastering the art of prayer.

Heavenly Father, thank You for always being with me. Please remind me of Your presence throughout the day so I will always be lifting my thoughts to You. Amen.

God's Longings for Your Prayers

Have you ever felt inadequate about your prayer life? Have you wished you were better at prayer?

First, know that God isn't looking for polished prayers. What counts is having a transparent heart that communicates honestly and freely with Him. That said, however, it *is* possible to grow in prayer. Consider this: How did you become good at catching a ball, riding a bicycle, or mastering some other skill? You learned by doing. So it is with prayer—you learn to pray by praying.

The more you pray, the more of a comfortable habit it becomes. As with anything else, this takes time. Don't feel shy about praying. God longs to hear you. Come to Him often, and you'll feel more and more at ease in prayer

Father, I admit I'm still learning how to pray, and my faith is often weak. Strengthen me by Your Spirit so I can communicate with You more effectively. Amen.

A Way
of Life

The Bible calls us to a lifestyle of constant prayer. We are commanded to "pray without ceasing" (1 Thessalonians 5:17). And because we have the Holy Spirit living in us and He knows what we should pray for (Romans 8:26-27), we can be purposefully praying at all times, in every place. When it comes to praying continually, here are a few time-honored suggestions:

- Start where you are. Even prayers of just a few minutes are great. The key is making it a habit.
- Start with your priorities. Pray for your spiritual growth, then your wife and family, and outward from there.
- Start with a prayer list. Jot down prayer requests on three-by-five cards so you can remember them and lift them up throughout the day.

Lord, to be able to talk with You anytime—all the time!—is such a privilege. Help me to take advantage of this tremendous opportunity and grow in my relationship with You. Amen.

A Man of Praise

What usually comes to mind when you think about David? If you're like me, you tend to think about his manly achievements. He fought a lion and a bear. He felled a giant. He was a mighty man of war. And he was one of the greatest kings of the ancient world. He was a man's man, a leader's leader, and a warrior's warrior.

Yet David also had a tender heart toward God. All through the book of Psalms he verbalized his love for God, praising Him and setting a good example for us. As a man who loves God, you should not hesitate to praise the Lord. Throughout each day, wherever you are, you should want to continually offer up praise in your heart and with your lips (Hebrews 13:15).

God, I see that expressing my love and devotion to You is the key to being a man after Your own heart. Today I choose to praise You morning, noon, and night. Amen.

Resting in
God's Power

Do you have a problem today—a challenge you are facing, something at work you must resolve, an issue with your wife or a child or someone else? Then help yourself to God's power as promised in Philippians 4:13: "I can do all things through Christ who strengthens me."

This one mighty truth can give you the confidence you need for finding the right solution to a problem and carrying it out. And as you do, you'll want to make sure you express your gratitude to God in praise. Now, praise isn't an activity limited to life's positive moments—you can also thank God in the hard times. Looking to Him with praise even when life is rough will help you to maintain a right perspective no matter what happens.

God, please remind me of this promise often. When I doubt, help me to believe; when I am afraid, help me to trust in You. This is my confession today: You are my strength. Amen.

Everything
You Need

The apostle Paul boldly declared, "God shall supply all your need according to His riches in glory by Christ Jesus" (Philippians 4:19). What a wonderful God we have! He promises to provide for all our needs, not *out* of His riches, but *according* to His riches. Do you see the difference? God gives in proportion to the immensity of His eternal wealth—that is, He gives generously.

You and I have much to praise God for as we experience His glorious provision day by day. If you ever find yourself wondering what to praise God for, consider what He has given you. This includes your spiritual blessings, both those you enjoy now and those awaiting you in heaven. As 2 Peter 1:3 says, "His divine power has given to us *all* things that pertain to life and godliness."

> *Lord, Your resources are unlimited—the well will never run dry! You've given me all I need for life and godliness, and You'll supply my daily needs so I can accomplish Your will. Thank You!*

With You Always

Do you praise God for the fact He is with you at all times?

In Psalm 139:7-10, David spoke in awe about God's constant presence: "Where can I go from Your Spirit? Or where can I flee from Your presence? If I ascend into heaven, You are there; if I make my bed in hell, behold, You are there. If I take the wings of the morning, and dwell in the uttermost parts of the sea, even there Your hand shall lead me."

It doesn't matter where you go—God is with you. Knowing that can serve as a great source of comfort, for it means you're never alone. This is yet another thing you can praise God for—that He is with you always.

Father, knowing that You are always with me makes all the difference. I'm amazed that You never give up on me and never leave me alone. I praise You for Your never-ending love! Amen.

Protection You Can Count On

Have you ever praised God for His protection in your life? Maybe you can recall specific times in the past when you've sensed God's protective care. It's also possible there have been times the Lord has shielded you from danger and you simply weren't aware of it.

David faced life-threatening dangers. Among them were the times that King Saul, David's predecessor to the throne, tried to kill him. Yet even in those circumstances David could pen this well-known verse: "Though I walk through the valley of the shadow of death, I will fear no evil; for You are with me" (Psalm 23:4). What peace is ours when we understand we are under God's protective hand! The next time you sense fear, remember that God protects you, and praise Him for His care.

God, You have protected me and saved me from disaster more times than I will ever know. Thank You! Help me to live in the humble confidence that You are watching over me. Amen.

The Habit of Praise

For too many Christians, the activity of praising God is limited to Sunday worship services or similar group settings. Yet God is worthy of our praise at all times. In fact, the Bible calls us to make praise a regular habit. In Psalm 34:1, David wrote, "I will bless the LORD at all times; His praise shall continually be in my mouth." And he said, "From the rising of the sun to its going down the LORD's name is to be praised" (Psalm 113:3).

Praise is a positive, God-centered activity that will affect and bless your heart. As you practice praising the Lord, you'll see a difference in your attitude toward your day. And others, as a result, will have a different attitude toward you and your God.

Lord, help me to be a man of praise. Guard my heart, my mind, and my lips so that whenever I'm tempted to complain, I look instead for reasons to praise You. Amen.

Making Worship
a Priority

From the beginning of the church, believers have gathered to worship God through singing, studying the Word, and celebrating the Lord's resurrection. Among the reasons we need to participate in corporate worship is that it provides the only opportunity during the week for fellow believers to gather and hear God's Word taught and then reinforced through "exhorting one another" toward "love and good works" (Hebrews 10:24-25).

Because everyone in your family needs spiritual nourishment and stimulation, you must take leadership in making church attendance happen. It's *your* responsibility as a husband, father, and God-ordained leader of your family to nurture the spiritual needs of your wife and children. So look forward to Sunday with anticipation, and use the weekdays to prepare yourself and your family for worshiping God in His house, the church.

> *God, so many good things happen when we join with other believers in worship. Help me to make this a priority for my family and to join whole-heartedly in the life of the church. Amen.*

Cultivating a Servant's Heart

As fleshly humans, our natural (and selfish) tendency is to take care of ourselves first. We like to make sure we've addressed our own needs. Then if we have any time or energy left over, we might be willing to use it to serve others.

But you and I need to resist those selfish tendencies and strive instead to live as servants. Many of the great men in the Bible were servants, including Abraham (Genesis 26:24), Joshua (Joshua 24:29), David (2 Samuel 7:5), and Paul (Romans 1:1). And Christ is our supreme example—He "did not come to be served, but to serve" (Matthew 20:28).

As you take delight in serving, you'll find yourself wanting to help others more and more. And they, in turn, will see Christ on display in your life.

Jesus, You are the Lord of all creation, yet You didn't come to be served, but to serve. Open my eyes so I can see opportunities to serve others and thus be more like You. Amen.

A Man of Your Word

I can't remember much about my wedding or what was said during the ceremony—it's all a blur in my mind. What about you? Since that day, have you thought back on the vows you made to your bride?

What's ironic about our tendency to forget about our vows is that they're among the most important words we've ever said. These promises were made not only before people, but before God. I'm sure you sincerely meant every promise you made to your bride on that day. What's important right now is for you to think about ways you can fulfill your vows daily. Won't you take a moment to pray and ask the Lord to help you recommit to carrying out those vows?

God, help me to be a man of my word and especially to follow through on the vows I made to my wife. Make me aware of opportunities to be the husband I promised to be. Amen.

A Noble Calling

God's call for husbands to love their wives is a noble calling—so much so, the Bible says we are to love our wives in the same way Christ loves the church. Jesus is our supreme example when it comes to how we demonstrate love, and the apostle Paul describes that love for us in Ephesians 5:22-33: It is sacrificial, purifying, nurturing, enduring, and active. So biblical love goes beyond mere words and emotions. It extends to our actions and includes a willingness to sacrifice one's self. In fact, Christ's love for the church was so great He was willing to die for her.

If you've felt inadequate about your ability to show such love, that's okay—humanly speaking, it's impossible to do. But with God's help, *all* things are possible. Ask, and He will gladly enable you.

Jesus, today I ask for a miracle: Empower me to love my wife the way You love the church. I repent of selfishness. Renew my thinking when I face opportunities to sacrifice for my wife. Amen.

A Sacrificial Love

What are some ways you can actively show a Christlike love to your dear wife? Biblically speaking, love is willing to sacrifice one's self for the benefit of another. This may mean giving up your time, attention, or energy—going out of your way or enduring inconvenience.

One big way to do this is to take care of the kids. You could babysit them for a Saturday while your wife goes to a woman's seminar or retreat. Or you could make breakfast for the children so she can sleep in. Or you could watch the kids one evening a week so your wife can take a Bible class. Or what about hiring a babysitter and taking a class together? In all these ways you can give your wife a much-needed break...and build better relationships with your kids.

God, sometimes the little sacrifices are the hardest to make! Help me to see small inconveniences as opportunities to be like You and to love my wife more effectively. Amen.

Encouraging
Your Beloved

In Ephesians 5:29 we read that husbands are to nourish and cherish their wives, "just as the Lord does the church." What encouragement can you give to your wife today in the things of God and her spiritual advancement? In her efforts at managing the home? In her personal growth?

If you see opportunities for your wife to develop herself or her areas of giftedness, make it possible for her to take advantage of them. This might mean letting her take a class, giving her a book to read, or letting her get involved in a church group. It may require time and expense, but if it helps your wife to grow, then you and your family will benefit. Remember, this is what Christlike love is all about!

Lord, You are constantly transforming and renewing our lives. Help me to cooperate with You and encourage my wife as You bless her with opportunities to mature and grow. Amen.

A Lifelong Blessing

As a runner, I can definitely tell you there's a vast difference between a sprint and a marathon. And marriage, of course, is a marathon. Your commitment to your wife is not for a mere 100 yards. No, it's for an eternity (which is what running the 26 miles and 385 yards of a marathon can feel like!).

In the same way that a distance runner has to endure difficulty and pain, you can't let yourself get discouraged by the challenges that come with married life. The permanent nature of your marriage vows means you stay with it for the long haul. This is the kind of perseverance God blesses. And when that happens, you'll find yourself enjoying the race, never wanting it to end. (Talk about a "runner's high"!)

God, thank You for the privilege of enjoying a lifelong relationship with my wife. Help me to cherish her as a gift from You that grows more precious with the passing of time. Amen.

Keeping the Spark Aflame

When you were courting the woman who became your wife, did you strive to be her best friend? I'm sure you did! You enjoyed being in her company, and probably wanted to spend every waking moment together.

But after marriage, for some reason that thrill seems to fade away, doesn't it? The demands of everyday life have distracted you, and you haven't done what it takes to keep the spark of your relationship aflame.

How can you recapture the joy you knew while you were dating? Think back on those days. What did you do to nurture your relationship with your wife-to-be? Make a commitment now to do some of those activities again. After all, next to your relationship with God, your wife's friendship is the greatest treasure you possess.

Lord, I repent today for not always nurturing my friendship with my wife. Thank You for her, for the blessing of being married to her, and for the tremendous possibilities our relationship holds! Amen.

Keeping First Things First

Have you grown so accustomed to your wife that you take her for granted? Would you rather be with the guys at a ball game? Or out fishing or golfing? Or working late at the office? (Warning: Don't answer these questions!)

Most likely, because of your everyday obligations, you don't have much time together—perhaps a bit before work, and a bit after. That doesn't allow for much alone time. If you find yourself wanting to do something other than spend time with your wife, in essence you're saying she's no longer a priority to you. That shouldn't be, for she is God's gift to you. So make sure to carve out time just for her, even if it means a personal sacrifice on your part (one you should make willingly!).

Father, I admit that I have sometimes taken my wife for granted. Help me to treasure her, to prioritize time with her, and to find creative ways to refresh our relationship. Amen.

The Pleasure of
Her Company

One way you can prove your love for your wife is
by taking her out on a date each week—going out
for dinner, going for a drive somewhere, doing something you both enjoy. Don't count the occasions when
you're invited out or entertaining others. And don't
let your children or work get in the way of a weekly
opportunity to show your wife you still love her.

One date a week can mean a lot over the lifetime
of a marriage. In 15 years that would mean 780 times
spent together without interruptions and distractions. Don't you think that kind of alone time would
make a difference in your relationship? The dates
don't have to be elaborate or expensive. Just making
time to enjoy each other's company is what counts.

*Jesus, You spent time with Your disciples and
ministered to individuals. How could I not
spend time alone with my lifelong partner and
best friend? Help us enjoy simple dates on a regular basis. Amen.*

Staying Focused

The mind is an amazing thing. It can carry on thousands of functions at the same time. That can be good and bad. For instance, if you're thinking about something else while your wife is talking to you, that's bad! There you are, looking right at her and nodding while she pours out her heart, yet your mind is miles away. You might try to hide the fact you're distracted, but chances are your wife will catch you!

When your wife is talking to you, the loving thing to do is to focus all your attention on her. Be all there for her, mentally and physically. This will take concentration and effort, but it's well worthwhile. You'll have a happier wife, and she will appreciate that you care.

> *God, today I confess that my wife is one of the most tremendous blessings You have given me. Help me to remember that when we're together and my mind starts to wander. Amen.*

The Art of Listening

I admit listening hasn't been one of my better qualities as a husband. I've had to work on this skill, and if the same is true for you, here are some suggestions I've found helpful:

- Realize that listening is an act of love. It says, "I value you and want to hear what you have to say."
- Make it a priority when you arrive home to spend a few minutes asking your wife about her day. Set aside all thoughts of work and give her your full attention.
- You know what it feels like when others don't listen to you. That's how your wife feels when you don't listen to her. So show her you care about her thoughts and feelings.

Lord, You always listen when I call to You. Make me more like You—attentive to my wife's voice and concerned about whatever is on her heart. Open my ears, Lord! Amen.

God's Charge to Every Man

When a husband doesn't provide spiritual leadership in the home, it affects the spiritual well-being of the whole family. In fact, it's why we see Christian marriages and families deteriorating at an alarming rate these days.

Are you determined to keep that from happening in your home? All it takes is a willingness to pay the price. It means not being selfish, and living out the responsibilities God has given you.

If you are married, God has placed you in charge of your family's spiritual condition. Your growth affects theirs. While that's a scary thought, it's an exciting one as well. God is ready to help you. And when you have a positive impact on your family, that impact will spread beyond the walls of your home and into the world!

Father, what a responsibility You've given me! And what a privilege! Empower me through Your Spirit to be a husband and father who glorifies You and blesses my family. Amen.

Loving Your Wife Spiritually

On your wedding day, you made a vow to nurture your wife. That includes both the physical and spiritual areas of life. How involved are you in your wife's spiritual growth?

Your assistance may be as simple as having a daily Bible reading schedule you follow individually then discuss together at the end of the day. It may mean studying through a book of the Bible together, or reading through a Christian book or study resource for couples.

Encouraging your wife's spiritual growth doesn't always mean having a part in the growth process. It can also mean being a "spiritual cheerleader"—coming alongside her to offer encouragement and support. In this way, you can fulfill your role as the spiritual leader in your home.

God, You want my wife to grow spiritually. Help me make that a priority too. Show me ways I can encourage and support her as she walks with You. Amen.

To Lead
Is to Love

Did you know that when you provide spiritual leadership in your home, you are demonstrating your love for your wife and children? When you take the initiative to lead, you are showing love.

Yes, it takes work to lead. It means figuring out ways you can help your wife and children grow physically, mentally, and spiritually. It means providing the kind of environment that enables them to flourish. It means time and effort invested in their lives. This is what it means to fulfill your God-ordained role as the leader in the home. It all starts with love—if you love your family, you will take the time to lead. Don't ever give up—your family deserves your best effort, and God will reward you for your labors.

Lord, do I reserve my best efforts for my work? For my friends? For my hobbies? Help me to see my family the way You do and to be a committed, creative leader at home. Amen.

Equipping
Yourself to Lead

The best way you can help lead your family is to make sure you are growing spiritually. This growth will give you the wisdom and strength you need for leading your wife and children. You can make this happen by…

- Reading the Bible daily so you are "complete, thoroughly equipped for every good work" (2 Timothy 3:17).
- Finding role models to emulate. "As iron sharpens iron, so one person sharpens another" (Proverbs 27:17 NIV).
- Avoiding negative influences. "Evil company corrupts good habits" (1 Corinthians 15:33).
- Avoiding tempting situations. "Flee… youthful lusts" (2 Timothy 2:22).
- Abiding in Christ so you can bear much fruit (John 15:1-8). This means praying to, depending upon, and actively obeying Christ.

God, please transform my family by transforming me. Speak to me through Your Word, through Your Spirit, and through godly men. Make me the husband and father my family needs. Amen.

A Love that Never Fades

No husband wakes up in the morning and says, "I think I won't love my wife today." Yet by our actions or lack of actions, we may be doing just that. We may inadvertently choose not to love our wives by not doing something for or with them.

Don't let this be you. When it comes to love, you can't rest on yesterday's laurels. You're to love your wife on an ongoing basis. What actions can you take today to show your wife you care for her?

This can be as simple as writing a note to her, surprising her by taking over one of her responsibilities (such as the dishes), or encouraging her efforts at work or as a homemaker. Every day that you awaken is another opportunity to show your love in action.

Father, I often forget the power of simply loving my wife in practical ways. You have equipped me to bless her and refresh her and encourage her. Help me to do that every day. Amen.

Honoring Your Wife

Do you want to have an open line of communication with God? Then treat your wife with respect and honor: "Husbands...dwell with [your wives] with understanding, giving honor to the wife...as being heirs together of the grace of life, that your prayers may not be hindered" (1 Peter 3:7).

To show understanding to your wife is to consider her needs and help meet them. After all, she is an heir with you in "the grace of life"—that is, in the marriage relationship, which is the most intimate of friendships and provides the richest blessings you can know in life. When you offer loving chivalry and companionship, God promises your prayers will not be hindered. That should help us husbands realize how critical it is that we love our wives!

> *Lord, may I see my wife today and every day as my partner in the grace of life. We both need for her to be spiritually healthy. Show me how I can care for her effectively. Amen.*

What Kids Really Need

Many dads today, though they have children at home, are absentee fathers. They are everywhere except in the company of their children. As a result, boys grow up not knowing how a man should behave, and girls have little or no exposure to what makes for healthy male-female relationships.

As a man after God's own heart, your marching order for parenting is found in Ephesians 6:4: "Fathers, do not provoke your children to wrath, but bring them up in the training and admonition of the Lord." You are to provide deliberate, ongoing instruction that equips your children to know and obey God. When you provide such guidance, you are loving your children as God calls you to. And you'll grow responsible, healthy kids who are a source of joy and blessing for life.

> *Father, help me to be the kind of person I want my kids to be, and help me to build a relationship with my kids so they want to follow me as I follow You. Amen.*

The Real
Thing

Can your children tell, by your words and actions, that God's Word has an effect on you?

Kids can quickly tell the difference between what is authentic and what isn't. If your life reveals you don't take God seriously, your children will notice—and they will probably conclude they have little reason to take the Lord seriously either.

How you conduct yourself has a very real impact on your children. That's why Ephesians 4:1 urges you to "live a life worthy of the calling you have received" (NIV). People are watching you—especially your kids. When they see you love God and desire to obey Him, they will realize your faith is for real. They will see God and His Word in a positive light. And that will encourage them to seek and follow the Lord in their own lives.

God, I want to be the real deal spiritually—for Your glory, for my own good, and so my kids can have a good example to follow. Thank You for my kids…they keep me honest! Amen.

A Key to
Successful Parenting

How you care for your wife is a major factor in caring for your children. Why? Because parenting is a partnership.

As you love your wife, you'll build her sense of well-being. This, in turn, enables her to better focus her attention on your children and have a positive influence on them. So by loving your wife, you are having an impact on your kids. That's one way parenting is a partnership.

When you work as partners, the task of raising children becomes much easier. So as you consider your responsibilities as a dad, remember that a key to your success is your love for your wife. Take a moment now to offer up a prayer of thanks for her, and make sure you affirm her daily as she helps you in the nurture of your family.

Lord, thank You for the partner You have given me. How can I be a better partner for her? Bless her today with strength and wisdom and joy and a sensitive, caring husband. Amen.

Having a Right Heart

As your heart goes, so goes your parenting. If your heart isn't right, no special parenting techniques or methods will help you. You must have a right heart before you can parent the right way.

And how can you grow such a heart? Jesus gave the answer in Matthew 22:37-39: "'You shall love the LORD your God with all your heart, with all your soul, and with all your mind.' This is the first and great commandment. And the second is like it: 'You shall love your neighbor as yourself.'"

Your love for God will naturally affect your relationships with those around you. If you love God, you will love your neighbor. And who are your closest neighbors? Your wife and children! So check your heart. Are your affections set first and foremost on God?

> *God, You and I both know my heart is prone to wander. Strengthen my heart so I can love You with all that is in me and love others as You make me more like You. Amen.*

It's the Heart that Matters

A child's behavior is driven by what is in his or her heart. That is, all behavior begins in the heart, whether good or bad. So all the training and discipline you give to your children needs to be directed to their hearts. When you shape their hearts, then you will shape their behavior as well.

Your children are given to you by God, and their hearts are your stewardship from Him. He expects you to do your part in raising them to know and love Him.

As you interact with your children, are you making a conscious effort to shepherd their hearts? Are you seeking to shape their inner person and not just their outer behavior? Focus on molding their hearts, and you'll influence their thoughts, words, and deeds.

Heavenly Father, I confess that I underestimate my influence on my kids' hearts. Help me to see how much my words and actions shape them. What a responsibility! Lead me, Lord, for their sake. Amen.

Taking Every Opportunity

Just before the people of Israel entered the Promised Land, God gave these all-important instructions: "You shall love the LORD your God with all your heart...and these words which I command you today shall be in your heart. *You shall teach them diligently to your children*, and shall talk of them when you sit in your house, when you walk by the way, when you lie down, and when you rise up" (Deuteronomy 6:5-7).

Did you notice the extent of your responsibility? You're to take every opportunity to pass on your love for God to your children—in all places and at all times. That may seem like God is asking a lot. But you're talking about shaping your child's life and his or her eternal destiny. So it's a task worth doing well!

> *God, make me a good teacher today—caring, inspiring, informative, fun. I'm teaching my kids the most important lessons of their lives, so transform me into the best teacher they've ever had. Amen.*

Raising Up Godly Kids

When it comes to influencing your children, here are the absolute essentials for every dad:

- *Love your wife*—When you love your children's mother, you love them as well.
- *Take your family to church*—This simple act is a giant step toward assuming spiritual leadership in your home.
- *Grow spiritually*—This is the only way you'll gain the wisdom and strength you need for parenting.
- *Spend time with your children*—Close relationships come only with time.
- *Model Christlike behavior*—Then you can say to your children, "Imitate me, just as I also imitate Christ" (1 Corinthians 11:1).

Lord, these things seem so simple, but You can use them to shape my kids' lives. May the things I say and do produce good fruit in them as they begin their own relationships with You. Amen.

When You're Overwhelmed

Are you feeling overwhelmed as a father? Maybe you feel inadequate for the task of parenting. Perhaps your children don't always cooperate with you. Or you've fallen short in your spiritual growth and you fear you're not the best example for them.

Whatever it is that discourages you, don't give up. God wants you to depend on Him for help. That's why the Bible says, "Cast all your anxiety on him because he cares for you" (1 Peter 5:7 NIV). And it's why we're told, "Trust in the LORD with all your heart, and lean not on your own understanding; in all your ways acknowledge Him, and He shall direct your paths" (Proverbs 3:5-6).

Give your concerns to God. Lean on Him and trust Him, and He will show you the way.

Heavenly Father, my kids need a better dad—one who loves wholeheartedly and serves sacrificially. Make me that kind of dad today. Cleanse my heart and renew my mind. Amen.

Do You Have a
Support System?

When it comes to carrying out the duties of fatherhood, there's great wisdom in seeking the help of a spiritually mature man who can give you guidance. When I first realized how much help I needed, I started looking and praying for someone who could assist me. And the Lord brought along a man who was a constant source of input that equipped me to do my job better.

Don't be too proud to ask for help. The stakes are too high. There is a spiritual battle going on for the hearts and minds of your children. Lift up your request to God in prayer. Look for a man who has his act together with respect to his family. Then you'll have a great support system for the challenges you face as a dad.

God, I do need help. Who can help me? What questions should I ask? Lead me, Lord, as I seek to become a better dad. Give me courage to reach out for help. Amen.

Making the Time

One of the greater challenges of fatherhood is finding time to spend with the kids. Most families are busy, and yours is no exception. However, busyness is not an excuse for failing to set aside time for your children. If something is important to you, somehow you'll find a way to make it happen, right?

So where do you fit your together times into an already-busy schedule? If you're like most families, breakfast or dinnertime are two key possibilities. Getting the time established might be hard. But once it's set and you're committed, you'll find it easier to make it happen. Don't betray your children through neglect. Be available to them. Outside of God and your wife, they're the most important priorities in your life.

Heavenly Father, have I neglected my kids? Help me to establish fun, meaningful, and regular times to connect with them. May my schedule be an accurate reflection of my priorities. Amen.

Consistency Counts

Through the years I've talked with many ministry leaders, including those on college campuses like UCLA. Frequently I ask them which students are the most difficult to reach for Jesus Christ. Without exception they have reported it is the children of nominal Christian parents. It seems the students from such homes wanted nothing to do with a faith that hadn't been lived out in their family.

This confirms that the greatest influence you can have on your children will come from your Christian example at home. The reality of Christ is nowhere better demonstrated than in your consistent, godly conduct. By contrast, inconsistency breeds confusion. So ask God to help you remain steadfast…for the sake of your children and their spiritual well-being.

Lord, the last thing I want to be is a lukewarm, compromising Christian. Today I renew my commitment to live in wholehearted devotion to You. Help me to live with purpose and passion. Amen.

Praying for Your Children

Providing a spiritual covering by bringing your children before God's throne through prayer is one of the unique privileges you have as a father. You may not comprehend what a rare opportunity you have until you realize that, with the exception of your wife's prayers and possibly a faithful believing grandparent's prayers, you may be the only other person on the face of this earth who is lifting your children up to God. Don't miss out on this blessed privilege! Pray for God's saving grace in their lives, for their spiritual growth, for God's continued working in them, and for their future mates.

O God, help me keep this as one of my top priorities! I am responsible to pray for my kids, and You will help me do that as I seek Your kingdom and righteousness. Amen.

Effective Discipline
Starts with Love

Did you know that when God disciplines us, it is a sign of His love for us? Proverbs 3:12 says, "Whom the LORD loves He corrects, just as a father the son in whom he delights." And Hebrews 12:6 says, "Whom the LORD loves He chastens."

Because God is perfectly just and wise, we can know His discipline is consistent and fair. And the discipline we administer to our children should be the same.

Kids usually don't like discipline when it's given. But if you make sure it's appropriate, explain the reason for it, and back it up with affirmations of your love, your children will eventually realize you have their best interests at heart. Those are the keys to effective and successful discipline.

> *Lord, I know You want what's best for me. May my children be just as sure that I want what's best for them. Each time I discipline my children, may our relationship grow stronger. Amen.*

Think Before
You Discipline

Sometimes in our zeal to discipline our children we can end up reacting to their wrong behavior in a harsh or inconsistent manner. If we're not careful, in our efforts to set things right, we can do more harm than good. The apostle Paul cautions: "Fathers, do not provoke your children, lest they become discouraged" (Colossians 3:21). To "provoke" means to make angry, and to "become discouraged" speaks of losing heart.

If you're too severe in your discipline, you can end up crushing your children's spirits, and they'll withdraw from you—until one day, when they are old enough, they'll just walk away. So when it comes time to chastise, make sure the punishment is appropriate and consistent. Avoid angering or goading your kids to the point they give up hope of ever pleasing you.

Heavenly Father, keep me from ever disciplining my children in anger. When I discipline them, empower me to use loving words and actions so they know how much I love them. Amen.

A Team
Effort

Earlier I said that parenting is a partnership. That's especially true when it comes to discipline!

It's important that you and your wife agree on *how*, *when*, *where*, and *why* you correct your children. You need to determine beforehand how you are going to deal with different types of wrong behavior. I'm sure you've already noticed that no two children are alike. Each child needs to be disciplined differently, and yet at the same time you need to maintain consistency. That's why it helps to plan ahead.

Another great benefit of making these decisions in advance is it helps your kids to know the ground rules—what makes for acceptable behavior, and what doesn't. This knowledge will encourage better behavior and greater harmony in your home.

> *God, lead my wife and me as we talk about this issue. Help us to give our children clear boundaries, enforce those boundaries fairly, and express our love consistently. Amen.*

Helping Kids Make Right Choices

The older your children get, the more they're away from home and exposed to the negative influences of the world. Which means there will come times when your kids are faced with choices and you're not around to give them loving guidance.

How can you prepare them to make right decisions when you're not around? One key way is to train their spiritual sensitivity so they can "discern both good and evil" (Hebrews 5:14). Equip them with the questions they should ask every time a choice arises. This will help them learn the skill of discernment. By helping them to evaluate the consequences of their choices, you will prepare them for a lifetime of making godly decisions on their own.

Lord, please help my children make wise decisions. Show me how to encourage their spiritual sensitivity and their desire to live in freedom and purity. Make them children after Your own heart! Amen.

Work Is a
Good Thing

Rumor has it that work is a consequence of man's fall into sin. But work existed before Adam and Eve sinned. In Genesis 1, we see God at work creating the heavens and earth. And when God was finished, He *"rested* from all His *work"* (Genesis 2:3). We also read that God placed Adam "in the garden of Eden to tend and keep it" (2:15). So God modeled for us the inherent dignity of work. Then He assigned man, made in His image, to work in the garden. So work is a good thing. It was created by God, and through it we are blessed to be able to provide for our families and contribute to society. What are some other benefits of work that you can thank God for right now?

Jesus, You said Your Father gave You work to do. I believe my work is part of Your plan for my life too, so I embrace it wholeheartedly. Thank You for the privilege of working. Amen.

The Profit of Work

Have you ever noticed that our physical and mental makeup thrives on work? We derive great satisfaction from a job well done. That's because God created us to be workers. In fact, the Bible repeatedly affirms the value and importance of work. For example, in Proverbs 12:11 we read, "Those who work their land will have abundant food" (NIV). Proverbs 14:23 says, "All hard work brings a profit, but mere talk leads only to poverty" (NIV). And the New Testament proclaims, "If anyone will not work, neither shall he eat" (2 Thessalonians 3:10).

God knows what is best for you. He ordained that you be productive through work. That should help you to have a positive attitude toward your job, which, in turn, can have a positive effect on all your co-workers.

> *God, help me to approach my work with enthusiasm and energy. May my commitment to be a good employee be a blessing to my company, my supervisor, and my co-workers. Amen.*

Your Job Is
God's Calling

What do you picture when you hear the word *calling*? Most of us immediately think of some form of vocational ministry. You often hear a pastor or missionary say, "I was called into the ministry." In 1 Corinthians 1:1, Paul said he was "called" to be an apostle. But what if I were to say that your vocation—the job you have right now—is a calling as well?

Wherever God has placed you in life—whether you are a painter, mechanic, soldier, salesperson, manager, teacher, or technician—that is not just merely a job, but a calling. It's where God wants to use you. What a difference it makes in your attitude to know you have the honor of serving the living God at your workplace and bringing glory to Him there!

Lord, thank You for giving me a calling and for empowering me to fulfill it. When my work seems uninspiring, help me to see it as an opportunity to glorify You. Amen.

Representing Christ on the Job

At your workplace, do you see yourself as Christ's ambassador? An ambassador is one who represents another—for example, the word is used to speak of a representative from one country to another. So being an ambassador for Christ means properly representing Him in whatever you do, including at work. You represent God as you go about doing your job.

What kind of ambassador are you? Matthew 5:14, 16 says, "You are the light of the world...Let your light so shine before men, that they may see your good works and glorify your Father in heaven." No matter how difficult or challenging your workload or workplace environment, every day is an exciting new opportunity to give the people around you a positive representation of God and the Christian life.

> *God, help me to see myself as Your ambassador to my workplace. May I represent You well— by humbly serving others and by performing my assigned tasks with excellence and joy. Amen.*

The Difference Christ Makes

A missionary from India told me about an army officer who stopped to have his shoes shined by a poor Indian boy. The lad launched into his task with such vigor that the man was amazed. Instead of the usual slipshod performance, the boy worked diligently until the leather sparkled with a brilliant luster.

"Why are you taking so much time to polish my boots?" asked the officer. "Well, sir," was the reply, "last week Jesus came into my heart, and now I belong to Him. Since then, every time I shine someone's shoes, I keep thinking they're His, so I do the very best I can. I want Him to be pleased!"

Do you demonstrate this kind of diligence at work? Because of what Christ has done for you, how can you do anything less?

> *Lord, thank You for the privilege of working for You in everything I do. Empower me to remain diligent every day, knowing that I have the greatest boss in the universe! Amen.*

Serving as Christ Served

Jesus was the greatest leader of all time…and yet He was a servant to all. He said, "The Son of Man did not come to be served, but to serve" (Matthew 20:28). As Christians, we are to approach everything in life as a servant, including business, management, or whatever kind of work we do.

Why not follow Jesus' example by being a servant to those with whom you work? Here are some ways you can do that:

Go with a servant's attitude	Go to encourage others
Go to promote others	Go to ask, not tell
Go to praise others	Go to give, not take

Jesus, You lived in this world as a servant—how could I do any less? Please live Your life through me and help me to know the joy of being a blessing to other people. Amen.

A Positive Focus

You have a choice between two attitudes on the job. You can go with an attitude of *taking from* your work whatever is needed for your well-being. This attitude perceives the organization and its people as existing to serve you. Or you can go to work with the attitude that says, "What can I *put into* this organization or job?" This attitude seeks to make the organization better—cultivating a more ideal work environment in which others are helped to live more satisfying lives. If that is your goal, then you will bring glory to God by fulfilling the role of a Christian servant...the role to which the Lord has called you.

God, occasionally I seem to think it's all about me. Thank You for redirecting my focus. You will take care of all my needs, so today I'll focus on what I can do for others. Amen.

Learning and Growing

One way you can prepare yourself to do your best in the workplace is to be a learner. If you want to make progress and grow, it's essential you have a positive attitude about learning. By this I don't necessarily mean reading school textbooks or taking classes. Rather, I'm talking about doing whatever you can to improve your job skills. This might mean reading job-related books or journals, or going to workshops that deal with the latest developments in your line of work. It could mean seeking personal training from someone who is more advanced than you, or asking questions and learning from the experience of others. A great way to start is by simply asking yourself, "What new thing can I learn *today*?" Doing this daily will help you to stretch yourself...and grow.

> *Lord, when my job gets boring, help me to see the possibilities that come with continued growth and learning. Lead me to opportunities to improve my job skills and increase my productivity. Amen.*

The Source of Contentment

Are you feeling content about your job? Maybe your answer is no because you work with difficult people, or you've been treated unfairly, or you feel overdue for a pay raise.

But you *can* know contentment at work even when things are rough. When Paul said, "I have learned to be content whatever the circumstances" (Philippians 4:11 NIV), he was in prison at the time, possibly facing execution. Yet he was content. Why? His contentment wasn't based on *circumstances*, but on the *Person of Christ*. Paul wrote, "My God shall supply all your need according to His riches in glory by Christ Jesus" (Philippians 4:19). When you focus on how God has met your needs instead of on your circumstances, contentment is possible, even in a difficult job.

> *God, when I am discontent, help me not to blame others. Instead, show me how I can find contentment in You and let the joy of knowing You affect every area of my life. Amen.*

Working unto the Lord

If you are discontent with your job, you'll find it helpful to ask yourself these questions:

Why am I here? If you see your job as God's calling, you'll view it as a ministry opportunity.

For whom am I working? When you see yourself as working for God, you are free to serve others no matter how unreasonable or thankless they are.

With whom am I working? Every person at your workplace is an eternal soul who needs Christ. That makes your job a mission field.

What am I working for? Money? Prestige? Power? If you are working for any of these, you will never be content. Only when you work for God's glory will you know contentment.

> *Father, help me to answer these questions honestly. Where my thinking is distorted, renew my mind so I can think about my job the way You do. Amen.*

The Power
of Integrity

Are you a model of excellence in the workplace? One key element of excellence is the character quality of integrity. *Integrity* is defined as being of sound moral principle, upright, honest, and sincere. Of all the people in the workforce, we as men of God should possess integrity. This trait should be the hallmark of our business life. Others should not be able to accuse us of dishonest business practices. Instead, like Daniel in the Old Testament, we should be found "trustworthy and neither corrupt nor negligent" (Daniel 6:4 NIV).

When people know they can trust you, you're likely to be given greater responsibilities. And even if that doesn't happen, you've achieved an even more important goal: You've given unbelievers the opportunity to view God and Christianity in a positive light.

> *Lord, do others see me as a man of integrity? Or have I compartmentalized my life, acting one way at church and another way at work? Help me to please You in all I do. Amen.*

A Man Others
Can Trust

We live in a day when faithfulness is viewed as an extraordinary virtue. However, for a Christian, it should be the norm. In fact, faithfulness is part of the fruit of the Spirit (Galatians 5:22). When we are fully yielded to the Spirit's leading, we will naturally exhibit this trait.

When a faithful person says he's going to do something, he does it. He doesn't make promises he can't or won't keep. David exhibited this character quality when he fulfilled his promise to protect Jonathan's son, Mephibosheth, after Jonathan's death (2 Samuel 9:1-13).

What would faithfulness look like in your workplace? To your wife? To your kids? Ask God to help you exercise this trait daily. He will honor your faithfulness, and others will be blessed by it.

> *God, help me to walk in the Spirit so You can produce the fruit of faithfulness in my life. Empower me to follow through on my commitments and keep my promises. Amen.*

An Offering to Jesus

There was a time when quality workmanship was the rule and not the exception. Now it's the exception and not the rule. As a Christian worker who represents the Lord Jesus Christ, you should want to give your best in every aspect of your job.

The next time you're tempted to cut corners or give a little less effort, remember that your workmanship is your offering to Jesus. Is it a worthy offering? Colossians 3:23-24 is a great verse to memorize: "Whatever you do, do it heartily, as to the Lord and not to men, knowing that from the Lord you will receive the reward of the inheritance; for you serve the Lord Christ."

> *Lord, remind me often that even when no one else notices the quality of my work, You do. May everything I do—including my tasks on the job—please and glorify You. Amen.*

A Passion
That's Contagious

How impassioned are you about your work? Do you approach each workday with an...

- eagerness to model Christ before a watching world?
- eagerness to contribute your energies to the success of your company or business?
- eagerness to contribute one more day's wages to the well-being of your family?
- eagerness to declare the praises of Him who called you out of darkness into His wonderful light?

When you're impassioned about your work, it lifts up others and contributes to a better workplace environment. And of course God will be glorified, which is your whole reason for being.

God, You have given me plenty of reasons to live with passion! When my energy is low and my work is uninspired, remind me of my high calling and the riches of Your empowering grace. Amen.

Loving the Church
as God Does

The apostle Paul wrote more books in the New Testament than any other writer. And aside from his consistent theme of salvation by grace through faith, his teachings on the church are one of the most dominant topics he addressed. That should serve as a clue that the church is an important subject. If God inspired Paul to say so much about the church, then clearly it is important to Him. So it should be important to you too.

As a believer, you are a member of Christ's body, the church (Ephesians 5:30). On a scale of 1–10, how much of a priority is church to you? What do your attendance, giving, prayers, and service reveal about the place the church has in your life?

Lord, thank You for reminding me how important the church is to You. I want it to be important to me too! Guide me as I reassess my relationship with the church today. Amen.

An Abundance of Privileges

As a part of Christ's body, the church, you enjoy many incredible "benefits" of membership:

- You were chosen before the foundation of the world (Ephesians 1:4).
- You were adopted as a son—you are a child of God (verse 5).
- Your sins have been forgiven (verse 7).
- You have been given a divine inheritance (verse 11).
- You were sealed in Christ by the Holy Spirit, which gives assurance of your salvation and eternal life (verse 13).

That list covers only the first 13 verses of Ephesians 1! Many more privileges are listed in the New Testament. As a member of Christ's church, you have been given much!

Jesus, help me to never take for granted the wonderful privilege of being a member of Your church. Thank You for creating a body of believers—Your body!—and including me. Amen.

Doing
Your Part

While membership in the church gives us many privileges, it also comes with many responsibilities. Here is a partial list as given in Ephesians:

- You are to live worthy of your calling (4:1).
- You are to be humble and gentle, bearing with others in love (4:2).
- You are to let your church leaders train you for works of service for the good of all (4:11-13).
- You are to put on the new self, created to be like God in true righteousness and holiness (4:24).

You have your work cut out for you, don't you? Fortunately God is gracious and patient, and helps you every step of the way.

God, I could never fulfill these responsibilities on my own. But I will cooperate with You as You transform my life and empower me to live as a member of Your church. Thank You!

Active
Versus Passive

For many years I lived a lukewarm form of Christianity with little or no involvement in a local church. Call it drifting, call it distraction, or even sin. My heart was not consumed with the things of the Lord. Then a dynamic Christian man ignited in me a new passion for God, His Word, and the church. I began to grow, and the results were life-changing not only for me but also my family. We gained many new friends who cared for and helped us, and now we're actively engaged in serving others.

Church can do that for your family too. Christ is calling for you to be active. Developing a passion for the church is a matter of obedience, which leads to many blessings. So determine to have a passion for the church!

Lord, thank You for reminding me that a lack-adaisical attitude about the church is sinful. I want to be passionate about the church because I want to be passionate about You. Help me, Lord. Amen.

Worshiping God Together

If worshiping God and growing spiritually are priorities in your life, you will attend church faithfully on Sunday. You'll also take advantage of other opportunities for spiritual input, such as classes or seminars for men or couples.

You and your family can never get too much input from God's Word! A wise man seeks wisdom (Proverbs 15:14), and that wisdom is available at your local church. Do you want to be a better spiritual leader for your family? The mere act of faithfully attending church with your wife and kids will go a long way toward making that happen. Your family will benefit as you grow more mature in the faith, and you will enjoy the fruit of their spiritual growth as well.

> *God, sometimes "becoming a spiritual leader" sounds like a lofty, nebulous goal. But faithfully taking my family to church—I can do that! Help me to take this practical step toward spiritual maturity. Amen.*

Riches
for Eternity

In the Bible, Jesus spoke frequently about money. Why? Not because the God who created all things needs our resources—it all came from Him anyway! But because we need to exercise care over our heart attitude toward money, which can easily distract us from the real priorities in life.

It's been said you can tell a man's priorities by looking at his checkbook. When you invest your treasure in God's church and people, that's evidence you have a true interest in the well-being of others. As Matthew 6:21 says, "Where your treasure is, there your heart will be also." Do your expenditures reveal where your treasures are? If they are in heaven, then you are laying up riches that will last for all eternity.

Lord, You know my heart better than I do. Thank You for reminding me that the way I spend my money actually shapes my heart. Help me to make eternal investments with my money. Amen.

A Cheerful Giver

If you haven't established a pattern of giving regularly to the church, you can start the same way Elizabeth and I did. We started with what we had, which wasn't much! And we began giving to the church from the front end of each paycheck instead of the back end. That communicated to God that He was our priority.

Have you asked God to help you handle your money with discernment? Ask Him to reveal any areas of greed or selfishness in your life. Your goal is to give with a cheerful heart. As Paul wrote, "He who sows sparingly will also reap sparingly, and he who sows bountifully will also reap bountifully...for God loves a cheerful giver" (2 Corinthians 9:6-7).

God, I've heard this phrase a lot, but today I wonder—am I a cheerful giver? All I have is Yours, and You will supply all I need, so I choose to give with a cheerful heart! Amen.

We All Need Each Other

At the time of your salvation, God gave you spiritual gifts. These are special abilities given by God and empowered by the Holy Spirit for the purpose of ministering to others in the church. God wants to work through you for the good of others (1 Corinthians 12:7,11).

Now, you can't mail or phone in the use of your spiritual gifts. And you can't delegate them. You must be physically involved for your gifts to be any use. Can you imagine what a church would be like if every member made use of his or her spiritual gifts? It would be a bit of heaven on earth. And it would be a powerful testimony to a watching world, which would see Jesus Christ through our actions.

Lord, I'm not very bold about putting my spiritual gifts to work, but today You're reminding me that I can make a difference in people's lives. I'm ready, Lord—show me the way. Amen.

Living to
Bless Others

When it comes to spiritual gifts, you are unique. Your spiritual abilities are an inherent part of your Christian makeup, and your giftedness is not like anyone else's.

That you are one of a kind affirms just how important it is for you to have an active part in church life. As Paul explains in 1 Corinthians 12, every part of the body of Christ has a vital role. There are no greater or lesser gifts (verses 15-27). So when any one person—including you—is absent, it's felt by the rest of the body.

What are some ways you've been blessed by the spiritual giftedness of others in your church? Thank God for the benefits you've enjoyed as a result of the Spirit's work.

God, thank You for the way You've blessed me through other people in the church. Help me to never take their influence for granted. And help me remember to thank them too. Amen.

Finding
Your Place

Have you figured out your areas of spiritual giftedness? Sometimes it takes a while to learn how you can best minister to the other members of your church. If you're not sure, simply start where you are. Do *anything* you can do, and do *everything* you can do, until you find *something* you must do. That something is probably your spiritual gift.

In time, as you allow God to work through you, you'll find the tasks ideally suited to you. Your spiritual abilities will rise to the surface more and more as you take advantage of opportunities to serve. Eventually you'll find your areas of greatest passion for ministry. That, along with your continued spiritual growth, will help to confirm the ways in which God has gifted you.

> *Lord, thanks for this reminder to serve others even if I'm not sure of my spiritual gifts. I trust You to lead me as I begin to fulfill my part in the body of Christ. Amen.*

A Right Perspective

When you are using your God-given gifts, others will be blessed. And you will feel blessed as you obediently and humbly minister your gifts. Yours will be the joy of knowing that you are fulfilling your special role in the proper functioning of Christ's body, the church.

At times you might feel like you're not having much impact. When that happens, remember this: All God asks is that you serve faithfully (1 Corinthians 4:2). It's not the size of your ministry that counts. Rather, it's your availability to God. As you let the Lord work through you, the Holy Spirit will make things happen. He will bear spiritual fruit. And one day, you will receive the ultimate reward—hearing Christ say, "Well done, good and faithful servant."

Jesus, when I don't see many results from my service, help me to remember that I'm ultimately serving You and that You will one day reward every good deed. Amen.

Hard Work
Opens Doors

I'll never forget a statement I heard in a class called "The True Masculine Role," taught by Bob Vernon, who at the time was a captain in the Los Angeles Police Department. He said, "If you want to be a good *witness* for Jesus Christ on your job, then be the very best *worker* on your job." If you've ever wished you could share your faith with others, hard work will pave the way for you. People are more likely to come to you for help and answers when you're the kind of worker they can look up to.

Bob's words had a long-lasting impact on my work ethic. Knowing that people are watching you is a powerful motivator for living in a way that enables them to see God in you!

God, I want to be a witness of Your saving grace. Please empower me to be a worker people respect and trust. Thank You for strengthening me every day by Your Sprit. Amen.

Being a
True Friend

One way you can "earn the right" to share about your faith in Christ is by having true concern for others. You may have heard the saying, "People don't care what you know until they know that you care." That's very true—your fellow workers, neighbors, and others must see you as approachable, caring, and friendly.

Before you can expect people to listen to what you might say about Christ, you need to build friendships with them. And as you become a better neighbor, you will earn the right to be heard.

It all starts with genuine caring. Show a real interest in what's happening in other people's lives. This will enable you to pray for them, know their needs, and be a true friend.

Jesus, You, the Creator of the universe, call us Your friends. Help me to pay attention to people and to notice when someone needs a friend. Amen.

Reaching Out

Real love always takes the initiative to meet a need in another person's life. That's the kind of love God showed toward us when we were sinners: "God *demonstrates* His own love toward us, in that while we were still sinners, Christ died for us" (Romans 5:8). Aren't you thankful that God took the initiative and sent His Son to the cross?

What a great example for you and me to follow with respect to those around us. Is there someone in need, a non-Christian you can think of right now, to whom you can demonstrate God's love this week? Perhaps it's as simple as offering a listening ear or an encouraging word, or maybe there's an opportunity for you to take actions that show you care.

Jesus, thank You for loving me and for demonstrating that love so clearly. I offer myself today to demonstrate Your love to someone You bring my way. Amen.

Loving the Unlovely

It's easy to show love to attractive or successful people. But Jesus commands us to love the unlovely, and even those who hate us (Matthew 5:44). Years ago, someone in our home Bible study invited a non-Christian woman from his workplace and, to his surprise, she came. This woman did not take care of herself—her hair was messy, her clothes dirty. Though she was unlovely, everyone endeavored to show love and care for her. She continued to attend, and in time, she accepted Christ! It would have been easy to ignore her because of her appearance. But we're called to love the unlovely, and let God do His incredible life-changing work in them. We are to view each person for what he or she really is—a lost soul in need of a Savior.

> *Lord, help me to look past people's outward appearance and to see their true worth, their dignity, and their need. You can meet those needs— sometimes through me. Amen.*

The Friendship Factor

Some years ago while in Taiwan I visited a friend I had known in seminary. He shared with me a couple stories that affirm the power of friendship evangelism.

First he shared about a man who hated Christians and despised the fact his son was attending a Bible school. One of the faculty members discovered the father liked tea. He went to the father to ask how he prepared his tea. Over time, as a result of this show of genuine interest, the father became open to learning about the gospel. The same faculty member also made friends with a local tea merchant. He dropped by the man's store for two years to learn more about tea. One day the merchant said, "You are different. It must be because you're a Christian."

Remember—no impact without contact!

God, as I make my schedules and to-do lists, please remind me to make room in my day for people. Teach me how to be a good listener, a compassionate ally, and a faithful friend. Amen.

It's More
Than Words

It is reported that the eighteenth-century French philosopher Voltaire said, "Show me your redeemed life and I'll believe in your redeemer." We tend to think of our witness as being verbal, but pointing people to Christ is not so much a matter of what you *say*, but what you *do*. You've probably heard the popular saying, "Don't talk the talk unless you can walk the walk." There's a need for your nonverbal witness (your actions) to back up your verbal witness (your words). To some people, your life—or nonverbal witness—is the only Bible they will ever read. So...what message are you conveying?

Lord, could my actions actually help (or hinder) people who are assessing their beliefs about You? That's more responsibility than I can bear... unless You live Your life through me. Amen.

Divine Encounters

One day I was stuck in bad traffic on a busy road. The cars were moving slowly, making me late for a meeting. As I inched my way forward, I spotted a woman standing beside a stalled car. I pulled behind her, found out her car was out of gas, turned around, and went to a gas station. Then I inched my way back to her car. As I left, I gave her my pastoral card and said, "If there's anything else I can do for you, let me know."

One week later she called for help with a family problem. After that, she came to church. You never know who the Lord might place in your path. Treat each encounter with an unbeliever as a divine encounter, and be blessed!

God, the next time I am inconvenienced by someone in need, please remind me of this story. Renew my mind so I can embrace these encounters as adventures! Amen.

Temporary Sacrifices, Eternal Fruit

How much are you willing to sacrifice to show friendship or concern to an unbeliever? It may mean having lunch with an acquaintance and listening to him pour out his heart (a sacrifice of time). It may mean inviting a fellow worker to a ball game and paying for the tickets (a sacrifice of money). It may mean inviting your neighbors over for a meal or dessert (a sacrifice of time and money).

Whatever the sacrifice, whether small or large, it will be worthwhile. How much is a soul worth? It cost God the death of His only Son on the cross. What's a few dollars or a little time in relation to eternity? Be willing to sacrifice yourself—God did!

Jesus, when I consider what You sacrificed for me, I can feel more thankful for opportunities to sacrifice for others. Thank You for the privilege of following in Your footsteps. Amen.

Living as
Good Samaritans

Some Christians have the mistaken idea that unbelievers are "the enemy." As a result, they have little or nothing to do with them.

In the story of the Good Samaritan (Luke 10:30-37), the Samaritan did not see the wounded Jew as his enemy, even though the Jews of that day were hostile toward Samaritans. Rather, the robbers were the enemy, and the wounded Jew was a victim. We rightly view victims of tragedy with empathy and concern. So why don't we view the unbelievers around us in the same way? They are the victims of Satan and sin (2 Timothy 2:26), and they can't help themselves (Romans 3:10-18).

Pray for unbelievers and show you care for them. Take every opportunity to be their friend and neighbor.

Jesus, have I passed by any victims lately? Open my eyes and show me someone today who needs my prayers, my time, my caring attention. Keep me from labeling victims as enemies. Amen.

A Willingness to Share

Men often tell me they don't know how to share their faith, or say they don't know their Bible well enough to talk to others about it. For these reasons, they shy away from opportunities for reaching others for Christ.

But it's not necessary for you to be an expert before you can let others know about the most significant aspect of your life. You already know better than anyone how you became a Christian, and how taking that step changed your life. All you need is to be willing to speak. God will do the rest, for it is His Holy Spirit that works in people's hearts.

> *Lord, the first step is always the hardest. Please help me notice opportunities to talk about what You have done in my life. And may my words always be filled with grace. Amen.*

Proclaiming God's Goodness

I don't know how long you've been a Christian, but you may have heard other believers talk about sharing your testimony, or your story of how you became a Christian. Even a new believer can do this, according to Mark 5:1-20. There we read about a man tormented by demons. Jesus cast out the demons, and the man was so thrilled he asked if he could follow Jesus. Our Lord didn't say, "Sure, sit at My feet and let Me tutor you for a few years until you are ready to share your testimony." Instead, He said, "Go home to your friends, and tell them what great things the Lord has done for you" (5:19). As a new believer, the man had all he needed to testify of his experience with Jesus. The same is true for you. Are you willing?

God, You have done some incredible things in my life, and I have no reason to be embarrassed to talk about them. Guide my speech, and use my words to help others know You. Amen.

The Bare Essentials

Your personal testimony can be broken down into three parts:

1. What my life was like before I met Jesus.
2. How I met Jesus.
3. What my life has been like since meeting Jesus.

Think back over the circumstances that led to your salvation, and the changes you've experienced since. Write out what happened to you. Once you've done this, you're ready "to give an answer to everyone who asks you to give the reason for the hope that you have" (1 Peter 3:15 NIV). Take a moment now to pray and thank God for your salvation. Then ask Him to give you an opportunity this week to share with someone else the reason for your hope.

Lord, thank You for giving me a story to share. As I look back on the way You've changed my life, help me talk about my story in a way that leads others to You. Amen.

Building Bridges

Become a neighbor. Develop friendships. Build bridges. *This* is what it means to develop a heart for reaching others. You don't need to be a pastor or Bible scholar to share your faith. But you do need to earn the right to be heard by those around you.

What are some ways you can build bridges that will help transport the message of Christ from your heart to the hearts of others? As you endeavor to live your life for Christ, others will see His transforming work in you through your positive attitude, pursuit of integrity, edifying speech, good work ethic, faithful church involvement, and a strong love for and commitment to your family. These can help open the door for you to build connections that eventually allow you to share about Jesus.

> *Jesus, "sharing my faith" sounds scary. Being a neighbor or a friend—I can do that. Make me more like You, so that when I'm around others, they want to learn more about You. Amen.*

God Will
Do the Work

Whenever you feel inadequate about reaching out to unbelievers, remember: Salvation is *God's* job. Building bridges is *your* job. And so is prayer. As you connect with people, you can pray for God to walk across those bridges into the hearts and lives of relatives, workmates, and neighbors. Pray for opportunities to communicate (Colossians 4:3), and pray for God to override your fears and give you boldness (Ephesians 6:19).

Are there people you can think of now whom you ought to pray for? Put their names on a list and pray for them regularly. Build bridges by showing you care for them. The time for sharing Christ might not come for a while—even a few years. But if you're consistent in prayer, you'll be ready when the door opens up.

God, guide my thoughts now as I consider who to be praying for. Give me strength to keep praying through the months and years if necessary. Thank You for answering prayer! Amen.

Points of Interaction

You can build bridges with unbelievers in a number of ways. One is to invite non-Christians to join you in your hobbies and interests. This allows you to have a point of common interest. You can also "meet unbelievers in the middle." What do I mean by that? You will find very few non-Christians in your church. For the most part, you'll encounter them in your neighborhood, your workplace, at the Little League field. Get to know people where they live and play. You could even become a coach for your child's soccer team or join an adult sports league. Both will allow unbelievers to see a Christian in action. Doing volunteer work in the community is yet another way you can serve as salt and light for the gospel. Can you think of additional ways to build bridges?

Jesus, You moved freely among people who were rejected by those who considered themselves religious. You loved them and blessed them...please help me to do the same. Amen.

Nothing to Fear

One common fear Christians have about sharing their faith is this: What if an unbeliever asks a question I can't answer? Well, hopefully there *will* be questions! Witnessing for Christ is not a monologue, but a dialogue. It's taking time to listen to other people's objections, fears, and questions, then seeking to give solid, biblical answers.

If you don't know how to respond, tell your friend you're willing to research the answer in the Bible, and set up a time to meet again. If you've done your job building the bridge, by this time the person should feel comfortable about getting together again. There's nothing to fear—God is with you, the Bible is your answer book. And the best part is that the rewards of sharing your faith are eternal!

> *Lord, thank You for taking the pressure off. I don't have to be a theologian. Help me be a good listener, a safe sounding board, a trusted friend... and a good researcher! Amen.*

Resisting Temptation

Of all the questions men ask me, most deal with the matter of purity. Today's culture has made it hard for Christian men to think pure thoughts and develop pure habits. But this problem isn't new—temptation has been around since the beginning of history. In fact, God faced these same issues firsthand in the person of His Son, Jesus Christ (Hebrews 2:17-18). And we're told victory is possible: "How can a young man cleanse his way? By taking heed according to your word...Your word I have hidden in my heart, that I might not sin against you" (Psalm 119:9,11). Victory is yours when you heed God and His Word. Spend time in the Bible and hide it in your heart, and you'll have the resources to resist temptation and stay pure.

> *Lord, when impure thoughts try to gain access to my mind, help me to fill my mind with Your Word. Lead me to passages I can memorize and call on when I need to. Amen.*

The Pursuit
of Wisdom

Where does a Christian man get wisdom and discernment? I think you already know the answer—from God's Word. And why is spiritual wisdom important? "That we should no longer be children, tossed to and fro and carried about with every wind of doctrine, by the trickery of men, in the cunning craftiness of deceitful plotting" (Ephesians 4:14).

Our wives, families, and churches need godly men who possess discernment—the kind of wisdom that can deal with life and its issues on a spiritual level. That maturity comes as you grow in "the knowledge of the Son of God, to a perfect man, to the measure of the stature of the fullness of Christ" (verse 13). Such maturity is *Christlikeness*—living and acting as Christ did. Doesn't that make the pursuit of wisdom attractive?

> *Jesus, You are the wisest man who ever walked on the earth. As I read the Scriptures, help me to think the way You do and to become more like You from the inside out. Amen.*

The Real Key
to Success

When you spend time in God's Word and grow spiritually, you are equipping yourself to make wise and godly decisions in all that you do. Joshua, who was Moses' successor, understood the importance of making good decisions. God told Joshua, "This Book of the Law shall not depart from your mouth, but you shall meditate in it day and night, that you may observe to do according to all that is written in it. For then you will make your way prosperous, and then you will have good success" (Joshua 1:8). Did you notice the key to real success? It's all about following and obeying God's Word. When your decisions line up with Scripture, God will honor you and bring blessing into your life.

God, whenever I think about prosperity and success, may I remember this verse. Remind me that blessing and obedience to Your Word go hand in hand. Amen.

The Right
Kind of Resolve

It's tough to make a decision that's unpopular, but Joshua wasn't afraid to do so. The first time the Jewish people had the opportunity to enter the Promised Land, Moses picked 12 spies to check it out. When they returned, Joshua and Caleb urged taking possession of the land (Numbers 14:6-8). But all the other spies lamented, "We are not able to go up against the people, for they are stronger than we" (Numbers 13:31). Joshua and Caleb were overruled, and God punished the Israelites for their lack of faith.

After his many years of service to Israel, Joshua told the people, "Choose for yourselves this day whom you will serve...as for me and my house, we will serve the LORD" (Joshua 24:15). Do you have the same kind of uncompromising resolve in your life?

> *Lord, help me to see what I'm really serving—money, popularity, myself...or You. Serving You is such a privilege! Please show me opportunities to be Your servant today. Amen.*

Sowing Good Seed

There's a quip that says, "If you don't like what you are reaping, change what you are sowing." If you find yourself disappointed or frustrated with life in general, then maybe you need to take a closer look at what you're sowing. Are you preoccupied with personal ambitions and self-gratification? Or are you focused outward upon God and the people around you?

God designed for Christians to experience satisfaction by pursuing Him and giving themselves in service to others. Romans 12:10-11 says we're to "be kindly affectionate to one another with brotherly love, in honor giving preference to one another... serving the Lord." When you sow love toward God and others, you will reap blessings. In fact, God will bless "exceedingly abundantly above all that we ask or think"! (Ephesians 3:20).

God, I don't often think about the kind of seed I'm sowing. Thank You for reminding me to sow good seed by humbly serving others. Guide me in Your steps today. Amen.

Marriage
God's Way

Marriage is a great invention of God. And a marriage where the husband loves his wife as Christ loved the church is a true witness to the reality of the Christian faith. But a marriage that honors Jesus Christ is not easy to come by. If you want this kind of marriage, you'll have to work at it.

God wants to bless you and your marriage. And He will, when you follow His blueprint for this sacred relationship. It requires having a heart yielded to Him. It requires a willingness to grow spiritually, which means spending time in the Bible so you can make wiser decisions and provide spiritual leadership. And it requires a sacrificial love for your wife. Yes, that's all work...but oh, the blessings that await you when you do marriage God's way!

> *Lord, today I affirm that a good marriage is worth the effort. Bless my wife and me as we invest our time, energy, and money into building a relationship that honors You. Amen.*

How Growth Makes a Difference

Committing yourself to spiritual growth can make an incredible difference in every part of your life. And when I talk about cultivating this kind of maturity, I'm talking about drawing closer to God, nourishing yourself from His Word, and yielding to His commands. When you do this...

- you'll grow in your ability to be a godly husband,
- you'll grow in your ability to be a godly parent, and
- you'll grow in your ability to lead.

This affirms a key principle we learned earlier: "Seek first the kingdom of God and His righteousness, and all these things shall be added to you" (Matthew 6:33). Have you taken that to heart?

Father, when I'm tempted to think I've traveled far enough, help me to get up and keep walking—closer to You, deeper into Your Word, and farther into a blessed life of obedience. Amen.

A Praying Husband

When you pray, you are acknowledging that God is an active participant in your life. Taking time each day to pray will strengthen you spiritually, and that, in turn, will strengthen your relationship with your wife.

You can go a step further by praying daily for your wife. After all, she is the most important person in your life. Place a photo of her in a place where you will see it frequently—on your desk, near your computer, or wherever it is you work. Then each time you catch a glimpse of her, remember to lift up a prayer for her in the midst of whatever you know she is doing about that time of day.

God, thank You for my wife! She is Your gift to me. Help me to treasure her by praying regularly for her and encouraging her as she grows more and more like You. Amen.

The Marriage Team

All through my growing-up years, I loved sports so much that I played in a lot of sandlot-type events. The teams were always organized on the spot, and winning generally depended on which team ended up with the best athletes. But sometimes when a bunch of average guys played well as a team, they would experience victory over the more athletic group.

This principle about winning as a team is true in marriage: Marriage works best when a husband and wife work in harmony. That's the way God designed this special relationship. And when you follow God's plan for working together as a couple, your marriage will be a little bit of heaven on earth. What are some ways you can become more of a team player in your interactions with your wife today?

Lord, I admit that I'm not always a great team player at home. Today I choose to follow Your direction as You show me ways I can be a better partner in our marriage. Amen.

God's Ideal Design

God created marriage. In Genesis 2:18 He said, "It is not good that man should be alone; I will make him a helper comparable to him." After the Lord created Eve, He then said, "A man shall leave his father and mother and be joined to his wife, and they shall become one flesh." In His perfect wisdom, God designed man and woman to complement each other and to enjoy a permanent and complete union with each other.

Whenever you take the time to nurture that oneness, you bring honor to God and acknowledge His ideal design. As you love your wife, you are showing love and obedience to God as well. And as a result, you'll experience the fullness and blessings that God designed for a married couple to enjoy.

God, "nurturing oneness" with my wife isn't something I think about every day. Help me to make that a priority from now on, and please show me creative ways to show her my love. Amen.

Everything You Need

In sports, equipment is everything. For instance, as a golfer, can you imagine having only one club in your bag? Or as a baseball player, what would you do without a glove? An athlete needs the right resources if he or she wants to do well.

The same is true about marriage, and God has given husbands and wives all the "equipment" they need to experience a great marriage. "His divine power has given to us *all things* that pertain to life and godliness" (2 Peter 1:3). Colossians 2:10 says you are *complete*" in Christ. You have every spiritual resource available; you lack nothing. And it's when you actively use these resources (such as prayer and the Bible) that you are enabled to enjoy marriage at its best.

> *Lord, I'm ready to quit making excuses and blaming others for my lackluster performance. You've given my wife and me everything we need to have a great marriage. Thank You! Amen.*

Fulfilling Your Role

For a sports team to win, every member has to perform well at his or her role. It's one thing to know your job on the team, but quite another to live it out. For instance, let's say I'm assigned the role of tackle, but in my heart I really want to play quarterback. That would create problems, wouldn't it?

When it comes to the marriage relationship, God has given the husband and wife distinct roles. When either of you step outside your role, you'll experience discord instead of harmony. To see how you're doing as a husband, read Ephesians 5:23-33. Are you providing loving leadership in the home? Do you love your wife as yourself? When you do, you'll work much better as a team!

God, You set the bar pretty high! But I believe that just as You have called me to follow Christ's example of loving sacrificially, You will give me the strength to do just that. Amen.

Two Are
Better Than One

King Solomon wrote the perfect words to sum up God's view of teamwork in marriage. In Ecclesiastes he wrote about the value of a companion—or for our purposes, a marriage partner: "Two are better than one, because they have a good reward for their labor. For if they fall, one will lift up his companion. But woe to him who is alone when he falls, for he has no one to help him up. Again, if two lie down together, they will keep warm; but how can one be warm alone? Though one may be overpowered by another, two can withstand him" (Ecclesiastes 4:9-12).

It makes sense, then, to purpose to work as a team in your marriage. And when you do, you'll not only be a team, but a winning one at that!

> *Lord, You are committed to my wife and me.*
> *Thank You for choosing us for each other. Today*
> *I want to show my wife how much I value our*
> *partnership, so please show me how. Amen.*

Seeking Your Wife's Best

Ever since Adam and Eve fell into sin in the Garden of Eden, it's been much tougher to know harmony in marriage. As fallen humans, we struggle with selfish desires and sin. That makes it all the more vital for us to examine our hearts, set self aside, and follow the apostle Paul's exhortation in Philippians 2:3-4: "Let nothing be done through selfish ambition or conceit, but in lowliness of mind let each esteem others better than himself. Let each of you look out not only for his own interests, but also for the interests of others."

As you both humbly seek the best for the other, you'll become "like-minded, having the same love, being of one accord, of one mind" (Philippians 2:2). You'll get a taste of marriage God's way.

> *Jesus, You never acted selfishly—not once! What are some ways I can look out for my wife's interests today? Thank You for giving me creativity and strength today to follow Your example. Amen.*

Real
Oneness

What happens when you work as a team to fulfill God's plan for your marriage?

You'll bring honor to God—The harmony and beauty in your unity will proclaim to the world the wisdom of God's plan for marriage, thus bringing honor to Him.

You'll bring honor to your marriage—A watching world will see your oneness and will want to follow your godly example.

You'll experience completeness—God's plan requires a husband and wife to work together, with each enhancing the other. As you each contribute your strengths and skills for the good of the marriage, you'll know true oneness. You'll feel complete as a couple!

God, You've given my wife and me a lot of good reasons to work together to follow Your plan for our marriage. Please remind me of these three whenever I think and act selfishly. Amen.

Setting Goals Together

To work as a team, you and your wife need common goals. Planning life together will give your marriage clearer focus and direction. How can you make that happen? Set aside a date when you can sit down and make plans for the upcoming weeks and months. Schedule the projects you need to do around the house, your vacations, special events with the children. Consider important financial decisions, savings plans, and so on. Set realistic goals as you put each item on your calendar.

After you've done this, you'll both know how to best coordinate your time and energy. Your plans will help you to have your eyes set on the same goals, making it much easier to work together and know success.

Lord, thank You for this reminder. Guide my wife and me as we share our dreams, set our goals, and make our plans. Help us glorify You in all we do. Amen.

Time
for Fun

Not only is it important to work together, it's also vital to have fun together!

The stress of work, everyday living, and taking care of the house and children makes it necessary for a couple to take a break every now and then. You need to plan times when the two of you can relax and enjoy yourselves. That may mean hiring a babysitter so you can have a night out, or getting away from the house for a change of scenery. Whatever you do, make sure it allows you to take a break from the demands of life and simply focus on each other. This will help you feel refreshed and reinvigorated, and will bring you closer together as husband and wife.

God, I need Your help. Sometimes I can't even think of fun things for my wife and me to do together. Lead us as we recapture the joy of playing and laughing and relaxing together. Amen.

Praying as a Couple

Not only does prayer makes a big difference in life, it also does the same in a marriage. Making time to lift your hearts together to God will take both your prayers and your relationship up another level. So carve out a time each day when you can go to the Lord in mutual prayer. It doesn't have to be long— even just a few minutes is good.

Praying as a couple knits your hearts together for common spiritual concerns and direction. Your wife will hear your heart as you talk to God, and you will do likewise as you listen to her prayers. As you continue to make this a habit, you'll find your desires becoming more and more fused together, bringing you closer as husband and wife.

Lord, You taught Your disciples how to pray simple, heartfelt prayers. Help my wife and me to keep it simple and to share our thoughts and concerns with You—together. Amen.

Swift
to Hear

Listening is a lost art. Too often we're impatient with others. We fail to respect people long enough to let them finish speaking before we jump in. We tend to value what we want to say more than what others have to say.

This problem is common in marriages. We become so used to each other that we don't listen as carefully as we should. We are so absorbed with our own thoughts or pursuits that we don't really pay attention to our spouse.

Do you remember how much you enjoyed listening to your wife when you first fell in love? Think upon your most recent conversations. Do you need to rekindle your listening skills? Do as James 1:19 says, and "be swift to hear, slow to speak."

God, do I interrupt my wife? Do I really take her words to heart? Help me to value my wife's words, to cherish her thoughts and feelings, and to show her how much I care. Amen.

Speaking
with Grace

When Elizabeth and I were first married, there were two topics we couldn't discuss without getting into an argument—religion and politics. Then, miracle of miracles, God came into our marriage and religion was the only thing we wanted to talk about!

Are there topics you and your wife avoid because they cause arguments to erupt? Together, identify those hot buttons right now and determine that, with God's help, you won't raise your voices or get angry when those matters arise. Colossians 3:19 says, "Husbands, love your wives and do not be harsh with them" (NIV). So commit to being a peacemaker. As Proverbs 15:1 says, "A soft answer turns away wrath." Bottom line? Speak with grace. *How* you speak is often more important than *what* you say.

> *God, I pray that today You will help me to value my wife's opinion. And when it's my turn to talk, may my wife always hear these words in the background: "I love you." Amen.*

Practicing Forgiveness

Whenever there's an argument between you and your wife, be quick to ask for forgiveness. Be willing to be the first to say, "I'm sorry." Rather than be a part of the problem, practice "sweetness of the lips" (Proverbs 16:21).

Now, some people assume that asking for forgiveness is the same thing as admitting you're wrong. But that's not true. Seeking forgiveness is not an issue of who is right or wrong. Rather, it's an issue of obeying God. Jesus said, "If you bring your gift to the altar, and there remember that your brother has something against you, leave your gift there before the altar, and go...First be reconciled to your brother" (Matthew 5:23-24). It is the wise husband who is willing to calmly settle or end an argument by asking for forgiveness.

> *Lord, please remind me every day of the difference between winning an argument and building a relationship. I know which is most important, but I need Your help to act accordingly. Amen.*

Earning
Her Trust

Trust takes years to obtain…and can be lost instantly with one foolish lie.

If you or your wife have ever been less than honest with each other, you know how hard it is—and how long it takes—to rebuild the shattered trust. That's why you want to do all you can to maintain honesty in your relationship.

And it's not just outright lies that hurt. Exaggeration, telling only part of the truth by leaving out certain facts, or being evasive and changing the topic so you can hide something are also forms of dishonesty that can do great damage. Speak truthfully, and you'll both enjoy the security that comes with trust.

> *O God, I see that trust is one of the most valuable but most fragile building blocks in our relationship. By the power of Your Spirit, I choose to be a trustworthy man today. Amen.*

Talk and Listen

Good communication takes time—a commodity that's all too rare these days. With your hectic schedule—and your wife's too—there doesn't seem to be enough time for meaningful talk.

How much alone time do you two have for communication? Consider yesterday, for example. If you had five minutes in the morning and fifteen in the evening, that's not much, is it? With so little talk, you could easily become strangers living under the same roof.

As you well know, you will *make* time to do whatever is important to you. To demonstrate your wife is a priority, make time to talk with her. Get to know what's happening in her life, how you can pray for her, what she's excited about or looking forward to. She will appreciate it!

Okay, Lord, I'll do it. Today I'll start setting a higher priority on face-to-face time with my wife. As I do, please help us to become closer than we have ever been. Amen.

Ending the Day Well Together

As fallen humans, we are basically selfish. Because of sin, we tend to have a self-centered preoccupation with self.

Therefore we husbands often don't show enough interest in what's happening with our wives. We're not inclined to ask about how their day went, how things went with the children, and so on. Instead, after a hard day at work, we feel like we deserve some rest and are entitled to relax or watch TV. We are ready to pamper ourselves—never mind the fact our wives have had a very busy day too.

That's why consideration is so important. A loving husband will ask how he can help his wife end her day more easily. He will lend a helping hand so that together they can rest when all is done.

God, thank You for my wife. I know she works hard. Help me to pay special attention to her, to pitch in and help, and to enjoy our times of rest together. Amen.

Real Love Connects

When you're tired, it's easy to make excuses for not taking the time to talk with your wife. You come home, slump down in the easy chair, and want to relax. You think, *I've talked all day on the job; I am drained and deserve to get some rest. Surely she will understand.*

Again, what you do in this scenario comes back to what's important to you. Yes, communication takes effort. But if you want to keep your marriage strong and show your wife you love her, you'll talk with her. You'll come alongside her and share what's on your heart, and listen to what's on hers. That's the kind of love God calls you to—a love that is willing to set aside self for the good of your beloved wife.

> *Lord, I know our marriage won't soar if I'm on autopilot. Help me to take the controls by creatively and purposefully connecting with my wife every day. I'm confident we'll both be happier. Amen.*

What Communication Does

Have you ever thought about the benefits of better communication between husband and wife? Here are some:

- Your friendship with your wife is strengthened.
- Misunderstandings are diminished.
- Peace and harmony are reinforced.
- Teamwork is enhanced.
- Learning is reciprocal.
- Intimacy is promoted.

You can probably think of more. Clearly, it's well worthwhile to make time alone just to talk!

God, if this were a cost-benefit analysis at work, there's no question what my response would be. Thank You for this reminder. May I be even more responsive at home than I have been in the past. Amen.

How Well Do You Know Her?

Listening is an act of love. When you listen to your wife, you are communicating nonverbally that she is important to you. You value her by valuing what she says. Your ears are your most important communication tool—so choose to listen.

Consider this from another angle: If you want your wife to listen to you and talk about what you think is important, then you need to start talking about what is interesting and important to her. What does she like? What has been on her mind lately? Make an effort to find out. Then you can be sure she will be all ears when you want to talk about Saturday's big game!

Lord, help me to become a better student of my wife. Prompt me by Your Spirit when I need to listen more carefully, ask questions, and just be with her. Amen.

Your Nonverbal Skills

Communication isn't always about what you say; sometimes it's about what you *don't* say. Just as there are times when you're not up to talking, your wife has times when she is tired, dealing with stress, or trying to catch up on a backlog of work. In such times, she might not be very responsive to you.

So look for those nonverbal hints from your wife that indicate now isn't the best time to talk. When you see those hints, save your conversation for later. And if you have time to lend a helping hand, ask your wife if there is anything you can do to help. That will let her know you're sensitive to her situation and that you care.

> *God, help me form new habits that show my wife how much I care about her. Thank You for giving me patience when I need to wait for the right time to talk. Amen.*

Wholesome Words

We might laugh when TV spouses exchange witty but nasty one-liners on a comedy show, but in real life, that kind of communication is no laughing matter. Criticisms and put-downs cause a great deal of damage and hurt, whether said in private or public.

A godly husband refrains from running down his wife, even jokingly. Ephesians 4:29 says, "Do not let any unwholesome talk come out of your mouths, but only what is helpful for building others up according to their needs, that it may benefit those who listen" (NIV). Always compliment your wife in the presence of others, especially your children. And never bring up her past failures. God has forgiven your wife, and so should you.

Once again, Lord, You have given me Your example. Your Word brings life; in some small measure, may the words that I speak to my wife do the same. Amen.

Your Wife, Your Friend

How would you define intimacy? If you're like most men (including yours truly), you will probably think in terms of sexual intimacy or lovemaking. While that is a part of intimacy, there's more to the definition. It also refers to great closeness—the kind that the closest of friends share, in which they feel they can talk about anything.

Are you enjoying that kind of friendship with your wife? Sometimes the friendship part of marriages goes through a dry spell, but this doesn't need to last. Purpose in your heart to cultivate *both* friendship and marital intimacy with your wife. Build the kind of relationship where she can say of you, "This is my beloved, and this is my friend" (Song of Solomon 5:16).

> *God, You can make all things new—including my friendship with my wife. As You renew us individually day by day, may our relationship also experience new life as we follow You. Amen.*

Alone Together

Intimacy happens when you and your wife take the time to focus your attention exclusively on the other. And it's privately shared, privately developed. That's why you two need to take time to be alone, rather than always doing things with other people. Your goal is to grow to the place that, no matter where you are, you feel a definite sense of closeness to each other.

If you desire this brand of intimacy, then you must start or continue building a best-friendship with your wife. Then I guarantee that both you and she will constantly be thinking of each other, and eagerly awaiting your private times together!

> *Lord, when it comes to intimacy with my wife, I've been thinking way too small. You have invested my marriage with incredible possibilities—help me to remember the sky is the limit! Amen.*

Where
Intimacy Starts

Every good marriage must, at heart, be a friendship between two people who truly care about each other. You as a husband must think as much of your wife as you think of any good friend, and even more so because you are life partners.

When you have that kind of close friendship in place, you'll find it naturally encourages a close physical relationship that fulfills each other sexually. In other words, intimate passion starts with the fuel of a faithful friendship, mutual respect, and clear communication. I once heard a speaker say, "If you want to have sex with your wife, be willing to go to the mall with her." When you are good friends, you'll enjoy a more intimate sex life.

God, help me to love my wife consistently—in our work, our play, our conversations, and our lovemaking. Help me to communicate my love for my wife in all I do. Amen.

How Talking Can Help

My personal opinion as to why sexual intimacy is such a problem for many married couples is a failure for the husband or wife (or both) to give careful consideration to the fact men and women are wired differently, and that is true when it comes to physical intimacy. When we overlook or refuse to accept male-female distinctives, we begin to develop faulty reasoning like, *My wife should respond the same way as I do when it comes to sex.* Then when she doesn't, we wonder, *What's wrong with her?*...and...well, you know the rest.

This brings us back to the importance of communication. The best way to better understand your differences is to talk. Doing this will definitely help your marriage!

> *Lord, I confess that I haven't instigated many conversations with my wife about our physical relationship. How can I help her feel safe enough to share her feelings with me? Guide me, I pray. Amen.*

Stirring
the Fire

Intimacy, for a married couple, is not something that just happens. It is hard work. Our fallen humanness has left us flawed with fears, bitterness, and selfishness. Our tendency is to look out more for ourselves than for others.

To maintain intimacy in your marriage means taking the time to build a close friendship and communicate regularly. It requires a decisive commitment on your part to stand watch over the fire of sexual intimacy—to stoke it, rekindle it, and do whatever it takes to keep it burning. Yes, this will require sacrifice on your part. But the incredible blessings that result from enjoying ongoing physical intimacy will make it well worthwhile.

> *God, You care about the level of intimacy in my marriage. I see that I need to make it a bigger priority. Help me to treasure my wife every day. Amen.*

Selfless Love

True, biblical love is a selfless commitment of one's body, soul, and spirit to the betterment of the other person. It is a love with actions, not just words. And this is the kind of love you are to offer your wife. If you routinely and repeatedly demonstrate your love by the words you say and by your actions, the intimacy God intended in your relationship will be forthcoming. No wife in her right mind could resist a husband who is giving this kind of love—Christ's love (Ephesians 5:25). She will freely share all with a husband whose chief goal in life is to sacrificially love her as Christ loved the church.

Jesus, no one has demonstrated selfless love as much as You have. And You want to make me more like You, so please help me use my words and actions to selflessly love my wife. Amen.

Equal
Yet Different

As Christians, you and your wife are equals before God. Galatians 3:28 says that from a spiritual standpoint, "there is neither male nor female; for you are all one in Christ Jesus." But when it comes to anatomy and physiology, God wired men and women differently because of the distinct roles He designed for them in marriage and the family. The man is to give strong, protective leadership, and the woman is to support and sustain life and living. These roles are taught in Scripture, and when we honor them, we will know completeness in the marital relationship.

Are you treating your wife as a spiritual equal? And at the same time encouraging her womanly distinctives? When you do both, you'll help her be all God designed her to be.

Lord, there is no one like my wife. Help me to cherish and nurture her tremendous gifts and wonderful distinctives. May I empower her to become the person You created her to be. Amen.

Purity

It's no secret that men can easily become sexually stimulated simply by looking at a woman. Therefore it's important that you monitor the "eye gate." Though you may have no intentions whatsoever of committing adultery with the body, you might just be committing adultery with your eyes. Jesus spoke about that when He said, "Whoever looks at a woman to lust for her has already committed adultery with her in his heart" (Matthew 5:28).

A key part of marital intimacy is purity. Your wife is to keep herself pure for you, and God asks you to do the same for her. In your case, that purity starts with your eyes. Make a covenant with God and let Him know you desire to monitor your eyes in a way that honors Him and your wife.

God, may I glorify You in all I do, including what I look at and think about. Help me to see my eyes as windows to my heart, and strengthen me to let only pure light in. Amen.

Guarding
the Gift

So much of what we see in our world today has sex connected to it. "Sex sells" is Madison Avenue's motto, and certain visual images on TV and on the magazines at checkout stands make it all the harder for a Christian man to keep his thoughts pure.

There is only one woman you are to enjoy in a sexual sense, and that is your wife. And if you remain faithful to her, you will know blessing and joy, according to these words from the book of Proverbs: "Drink water from your own cistern, and running water from your own well…Let your fountain be blessed, and rejoice with the wife of your youth…let her breasts satisfy you at all times; and always be enraptured with her love" (5:15,18-19).

> *Lord, the world has distorted Your tremendous gift of sex. Help my wife and me to enjoy the real thing by guarding our eyes and hearts and preserving the precious gift you have given us. Amen.*

Making Yourself
a Better Spouse

No marriage is all that it could be. Why? Because no person is all that he or she could be in their spiritual growth and maturity. That's what makes marriage a challenge!

Every marriage is always in need of fine tuning. People change, circumstances change, the makeup of the family changes. And the marriage must adapt. Your ability to adjust to the ages and stages of marriage will ensure stability, security, and intimacy. Ask God right now to open your heart to the changes you need to make in your life so your marriage can continue to grow. While your human tendency is to want to change the *other* person, God calls you to change *yourself*, and you are directly accountable to Him for doing what's right in the marriage relationship.

> *God, regardless of how good my marriage is, You have even greater things in store! I don't want to stagnate. As You are transforming me, I know you'll transform my marriage as well. Amen.*

Sexual Sensitivity

Sexual intimacy can become a major problem if you and your wife are operating on different schedules, especially when it comes time to retire for the evening. If that's true for you, make a concerted effort to plan with your wife to go to bed at the same time. A little thing like that can make a big difference in your sex life. As I've said before, intimacy doesn't just happen. Being close physically will generate feelings in both of you that wouldn't arise if one of you is still out in the family room watching television, surfing the Internet, or poring over paperwork from the office. Don't purposefully sabotage your sex life with late-night diversions. Make sure you work together at fulfilling each other's sexual desires (1 Corinthians 7:3).

> *Lord, when I read these simple reminders, I realize how insensitive I can be. Help me do the simple things, the right and true things that will build intimacy in my marriage. Amen.*

Looking Good

The Bible says that "the husband does not have authority over his own body, but the wife does" (1 Corinthians 7:4). This means your body is not yours. It's the property of your wife! Therefore you are to be a good steward of your wife's real estate by keeping your body well-groomed and in good physical health—not for your sake, but for hers. If you want your wife to be more sexually attracted to you, then do your part. While good grooming may seem a little thing, it makes a big difference. Shower when you need to, and take care of your appearance. Do what you can to stay in shape—exercise, take walks, join a gym. Losing a few pounds never hurts in the Lovemaking Department.

> *God, I confess that I've held a double standard, expecting my wife to be beautiful but not considering my own body. I repent! Help me love my wife by taking care of my body. Amen.*

Keeping the Peace

One very big hindrance to marital intimacy is anger. That's a key reason the Bible says, "Do not let the sun go down on your wrath" (Ephesians 4:26). In other words, don't go to bed angry.

Disagreements and spats usually fester and grow foul if they are allowed to continue unresolved. That's why you want to deal with them right away. A right relationship with your wife is more important than winning an argument. So restore that bond with your beloved with a willingness to say, "I'm sorry." When you pursue forgiveness and reconciliation, intimacy will naturally follow. So when conflict occurs, be sure to make up with each other quickly!

Lord, when I'm angry, prompt me by Your Spirit to express my feelings in a controlled and loving way. And when my wife is angry, help me to not take her feelings too personally. Amen.

Romancing Your Wife

One of the best ways to keep the fires of passion burning in both of you is to get away on a regular basis. If you want your wife to respond to you physically, then take the initiative. Find a place that's not too far away and not too expensive. (You'll want to do this again, so don't break the bank the first time.) Find a babysitter or arrange with friends to exchange child-care responsibilities. Getting your wife away from the distractions of the house, children, and a myriad of other things, even for one night, allows for a focused time together. A getaway every now and then will rejuvenate your sex life and enhance your marriage.

> *God, what have I been waiting for? More money? More time? I confess that these are lame excuses. Help me to realign my priorities and plan a romantic getaway now. Amen.*

Money Matters

If you were to ask most marriage counselors to identify one of the top, if not *the* top, causes of conflicts in a marriage, I believe the majority would say it's money—how it is acquired, how it is spent, and by whom. That's why as husbands we need to make sure we are giving strong leadership in our marriage in the area of money management.

This means you need to exercise self-control when it comes to handling money yourself. In fact, the way your children handle money will depend on the example you set, and whether you take time to teach them how to use it wisely. Your efforts may save you and your children much heartache later on. How would you rate the example you are setting, and in what ways can you improve?

> *Lord, help me to embrace this responsibility— to give, save, and spend wisely and to train my children to do the same. May money management be a strength and not a weakness in our family. Amen.*

God
and Money

If others were allowed a peek at your checkbook, what would they see? Checks written to missionaries, to your church, to charities? And checks toward the necessities of life, the needs of your family, your children's education? Or would they see a long log of checks written for indulgences, excesses, frivolities, and fun?

While your checkbook may be a private matter with regard to the people around you, that's not the case with God. He knows your every expenditure; He knows your heart attitude toward money. What do you think God would say about the way you handle your finances? This doesn't mean you can't have fun occasionally. But a man after God's own heart will make sure that true needs and priorities are taken care of first.

God, I want my priorities to match Yours. May my expenditures demonstrate that I trust You and that I care about the things You care about. Thank You for leading and guiding me. Amen.

On Loan
from God

The money and the things you own—who does it all belong to? Do you view your family, your possessions, and everything else as gifts from God that are on loan to you? The psalmist wrote, "The earth is the LORD's, and all its fullness, the world and those who dwell therein" (24:1).

So what then is your role? If God is the owner and you are the user, then you are a *steward* of God's gifts to you. And 1 Corinthians 4:2 says, "It is required in stewards that one be found faithful." How would you rate your stewardship of your family, your talents, your spiritual gifts, your body, your money? God rewards those who are faithful—so every effort you make toward good stewardship is well worthwhile.

Lord, everything in the world is Yours—including the things You have entrusted to me. Make me a good and faithful steward, I pray, pleasing You in every financial transaction I make. Amen.

From Want to Contentment

Contentment—or the lack of it—can have a major impact on how you manage your money. Advertisers say, "You need this new car," or "You deserve a luxury vacation." And if you're not content with what you have, it becomes all too easy to go into debt in order to get that car or go on that vacation.

Our sinful flesh fights against contentment and is prone to the "wants" of life. It's when we learn contentment that we are able to hold on to money longer and spend more wisely. And the more careful you are, the more your children will see the fallacy of society's delusion that wealth and possessions bring happiness. Contentment, then, is a significant key to good money management, and to the spiritual health and well-being of your family.

> *God, You have given me every reason to be content—and more! When my heart is restless, help me rest in You and enjoy the deep contentment of knowing that I am in Your care. Amen.*

A Right Attitude Toward Money

God doesn't want or need your money. Why? Because according to the Bible, He owns all the cattle on the hills (Psalm 50:10). But what God does desire in His people is an attitude of selflessness. The apostle Paul said when it comes to giving, "God loves a cheerful giver" (2 Corinthians 9:7). God loves and blesses the person who gives out of a heart of love, not out of the size of his bank account.

When it comes to giving, the issue isn't how much you should give to God, but how much of God's money you should keep for yourself. Everything you have has been entrusted to you by the Lord. What would happen if you made all your financial decisions with God's approval in mind?

Lord, I wouldn't always describe my attitude about money as cheerful. But I know that You will provide all I need, so help me adjust my attitude and give with a happy heart. Amen.

Giving as God Leads

There are many opinions about how much we should give to the Lord. What makes this hard is that every person has different financial circumstances and needs. Fortunately we find a helpful example in the lives of the Christians in Macedonia (in what is now part of modern-day Greece). They were poor and afflicted, yet they were rich in love and obedience. They gave selflessly and generously to God for the needs of others (2 Corinthians 8:1-6).

These Christians gave "according to their ability" (verse 3). That's a good rule of thumb to follow—we ought to give at least "according to" how we have prospered (1 Corinthians 16:2). Don't let others set the standard for you. Ask God to place on your heart a sense for how much you can give cheerfully, selflessly, and generously.

> *God, please help me stop comparing myself with others. Lead me as I consider how You would have me use the resources You have entrusted to me. I trust You to provide for me. Amen.*

Giving with Gratitude

Giving is a part of your worship to God, and giving sacrificially is an essential part of that worship. Has God blessed your life? I know He has, and so do you. Then why not show your love and appreciation by giving even more sacrificially? You cannot out-give God.

Remember too that salvation is a free gift God gives to us through His grace (Ephesians 2:8-9). And we have been given "every spiritual blessing in the heavenly places in Christ" (Ephesians 1:3). So when we give, we ought to do so out of a heart that is overflowing with love for and gratitude to our Savior, the Lord Jesus Christ.

> *Lord, knowing that You love and accept me even before I give a penny...that fills me with gratitude! I'm secure in You, so help me to give with joy and thanks. Amen.*

Keeping a
Single Focus

Does money dominate your thoughts and life? These questions will help you determine the answer:

- Do you think and worry about money frequently?
- Do you give up family priorities to make more money?
- Do you spend a lot of your time caring for your things?
- Is it hard for you to give to the Lord's work?

A preoccupation with money will affect your relationship with God. As Jesus said, "No one can serve two masters...You cannot serve God and mammon [riches]" (Matthew 6:24). So don't long for more money. Work hard for your means, but keep God first and trust Him to provide for your family's needs.

God, it's so easy for me to get distracted, focusing on money instead of trusting in You. Money is a cruel taskmaster, but You are my loving heavenly Father. I'd much rather serve You. Amen.

Real Satisfaction

When it comes to our finances, we need to follow Paul's example. He was able to say, "I have learned the secret of being content in any and every situation" (Philippians 4:12 NIV). Try learning how to say no to yourself in the "things" department. Try being content with what you have. Try being happy about what other people have. Try being content with "food and clothing" (1 Timothy 6:8). Try being content with "godliness" (verse 6).

When you are content, you will know real satisfaction—not only in the financial department, but the spiritual department as well!

Father, You have given me all I need for life and godliness, and You have added more blessings than I can count. I am content when I consider all that You have done. Thank You. Amen.

Passing Through

We as Christians are in the world but we are not to be consumed with the things of this world (1 John 2:15). We are merely pilgrims who are passing through (1 Peter 2:11). We are citizens of heaven (Philippians 3:20), and we are to eagerly await the return of our King to reign here on the earth.

One sure solution to worldliness is to follow Paul's admonition to "set your mind on things above, not on things on the earth" (Colossians 3:2). When you focus on God, His Word, and spiritual priorities, you're less likely to succumb to the lures of the world. So "seek first the kingdom of God and His righteousness," and He will take care of the rest—"all these things shall be added to you" (Matthew 6:33).

> *Lord, focusing on worldly things makes me anxious and discontented. But when I think about You and the tremendous work You are doing in and through me, I'm filled with confidence. Thank You!*

It Pays to
Have a Plan

Most financial planners say the starting point for good money management is having a budget. Without a budget, you can't plan ahead, and you may end up buying things that either aren't essential or will put you deeper into debt. A plan for saving and spending will provide you with boundaries that will help get your finances into better shape. And it will help you to differentiate much more wisely between real needs and mere wants.

The key to a successful budget, of course, is making it together with your wife and agreeing that you'll both abide by it. Then as you see your financial situation improve, you can celebrate and enjoy the benefits that having—and sticking to—a budget brings your way.

> *God, as my wife and I assess our budget, help us to agree on priorities that glorify You, bless others, and keep us free from the love of money. Amen.*

Seeking
God's Input

Since the money you manage really belongs to God, shouldn't you consult Him as to how you spend it? Hopefully you and your wife have already committed your budget to the Lord. Pray about your finances, and pray whenever it comes time to make a major purchase. Ask yourselves, "How will this purchase impact our budget?" And, "Is it wiser for us to repair the current car or appliance rather than buy a new one?"

As you prayerfully bring your financial decisions to God, you'll develop more and more of a steward's mind-set in all you do with your money. You're also less likely to make impulse spending decisions you'll regret later on. Prayer will help you slow down, make careful choices, and make the most of your resources.

> *Lord, guide my wife and me as we endeavor*
> *to bring everything in our lives, including our*
> *finances, to You in prayer. Help us to apply what*
> *You're teaching us and to make wise decisions.*
> *Amen.*

Compounded Blessings

There are many blessings that come with good money management. For example, being a faithful steward of God's money will result in *God* being glorified. Your *wife* will be blessed as you model self-control when it comes to the stuff of this world. Your *children* will be blessed and influenced by your financial leadership. *You* will be blessed by your obedience. And *others* will be blessed through your generous giving.

Talk about "compounded interest"! You'll experience "compounded blessings" as you are obedient to the Lord in this key area of your life and marriage.

Lead me, God. Show me where my financial management is weak. Strengthen my heart so I can trust You to provide. And teach me how to be a wise and faithful steward. Amen.

The Riches of Wisdom

The Bible repeatedly exhorts us to pursue wisdom. Simply defined, wisdom is the application of knowledge, and sometimes even plain old common sense.

How important is wisdom? Proverbs 24:3-4 says, "Through wisdom a house is built, and by understanding it is established. By knowledge the rooms are filled with all precious and pleasant riches."

Doesn't that make you want to grow in wisdom? The good news is God made it very accessible. In the Bible, we can find "all things that pertain to life and godliness" (2 Peter 1:3). So if you need wisdom as a man, husband, or father, turn to God's Word. In doing so, you'll build up your house and fill it "with all precious and pleasant riches."

Lord, save me from foolishness and help me to grow in wisdom. Please transform my mind as I read Your Word, converse with people who know You, and seek You in prayer. Amen.

A Godly Example

There is no greater treasure than a husband and father who models godliness before his wife and children on a daily basis. By godliness, I mean right conduct. In Proverbs we learn that "in the house of the righteous there is much treasure" (15:6). God brings blessing to the man who is a godly example to the rest of his family.

When you pursue what is right and honorable, your wife and children will know that your heart's desire is to honor God. They will know you're a man of your word, and that you can be trusted. This will provide them with a sense of security and bring stability into your home. Wouldn't you like to enjoy that kind of treasure? Then make godliness a priority in your life.

God, I don't usually consider myself a godly person. But You are transforming me, setting me free, and helping me to live the life You intended for me. Make me more like You, I pray. Amen.

Fulfillment
at Home

Most wives receive their greatest joy and fulfillment from their home. To them, home represents security, peace, and a sense of belonging. That's why wives often fuss with the house, moving things around and making things look nice. And that's why, when something is wrong and they can't fix it, their nature becomes unsettled. They need their "nest" made right.

So when something needs fixing around the house, the sooner you get to it, the better. Be willing to set aside your personal wants and show your wife you love her by doing your part in the upkeep of the home. Do this and you'll have a much happier wife, which, in turn, will contribute toward a happier marriage.

Lord, I know how upset I get when something important to me just isn't right. Please make me sensitive to my wife's feelings and eager to bless her by helping to make things right. Amen.

Praising God for His Gifts

When was the last time you thanked the Lord for the blessing of your home and the people in it? Don't ever take His gifts to you for granted. Love your home, care for it, and praise God for it. When it comes to thanking Him for what you have at home, you'll find a great example in King David, who said, "Who am I, O Lord God? And what is my house, that You have brought me this far?... You are great, O Lord God" (2 Samuel 7:18,22).

Does David's prayer and attitude reflect your heart? Can you humbly say, "Who am I, O Lord God? And what is my house, that You have brought me this far?" God has blessed you and your house; make a habit of thanking Him for all He has given you.

> *God, save me from ever taking my family or our home for granted. Even in our hardest times, You have blessed us with so much more than we deserve. Thank You! Amen.*

Handoff to the Next Generation

If you have children, your willingness to take the time to instruct them in the Bible will help ensure that the next generation carries on our faith in Christ. Moses said it this way to the Israelites before they entered the Promised Land: "These words which I command you today shall be in your heart. You shall teach them *diligently* to your children" (Deuteronomy 6:6-7).

The Hebrew parents were to make an all-out effort to pass their faith on to the next generation. And, Christian father, that is your mandate as well! Keep in mind that, humanly speaking, the Christian faith is only one generation away from extinction. So do your part to instill the Bible's teachings in your children, then trust God to do His work in their hearts.

Lord, I want to set a good example for my kids and talk with them about knowing You. Help me to know what they need to hear and how to communicate effectively. Amen.

Passing on Your Faith

As a dad, have you ever considered that you cannot impart to your kids what you do not possess yourself? Notice a parent's first responsibility, according to Moses: "You shall love the LORD your God with all your heart, with all your soul, and with all your strength. And these words which I command…You shall teach them diligently to your children" (Deuteronomy 6:5-7). Moses told parents to *first* love God themselves. Only then could they pass their faith on to their children.

Make it your chief aim in life to develop a living and growing love for God. Your children will notice this, and they will respond positively as they see what's important to you.

God, the last thing I want is to be a fake—someone who doesn't walk the talk. Whenever I'm teaching my kids, help me to look to my own life and make any necessary adjustments. Amen.

A Faith
with Impact

Your children must never for a moment think your faith isn't the most important thing in your life. They must never conclude that Christianity is only a "Sunday faith." Instead, they must hear you talking about Jesus. They must see the excitement you have for the things of the Bible and your heart's desire to love, obey, and serve God. And it's important you don't confuse them by engaging in behaviors that contradict your example as a believer.

On a day-to-day basis, you might think you're not having much impact. But as you remain consistent over the long haul, you'll cement lasting impressions in your children's minds. You'll help them to realize what it means to put God first and love Him with all your heart.

Lord, someday, when my kids leave the house and look back on our time together, may they see me as a man who loves You and endeavors to follow You every day. Amen.

Your Greatest Investment

Time is always in such short supply for us men! We never seem to have enough of it. We are usually busy every spare minute. And sometimes it's a challenge to make sure your children get some of that time.

When it comes to the priority of time with children, I often tell men this paraphrased quote from Jesus: "What is a man profited if he gains the whole world, and loses or forfeits [his children]?" (Luke 9:25 NASB). Your kids are worth more than all the material wealth in the world. So it's vital to set aside time for them. Every moment you spend with them accumulates to become your greatest investment and will reap wonderful dividends.

God, help me to create great memories with my kids—memories of fun times with a dad who would do anything in the world for them because he loves them and loves You. Amen.

Setting Things Right

You may have had times when you've felt utterly inadequate as a father. You've made a mess of things, and you've had your priorities in the wrong places. You haven't been the best example to your kids, and you might even feel like giving up on this parenting thing.

Well, if you're reading this book, that's a sign you want to do what is correct, so you're taking steps in the right direction. Your desire is to be a man after God's own heart, and that's what counts most. So ask God to forgive your past mistakes and to give you renewed energy for fulfilling your role as a father. As you yield yourself to God, He will carry on His work through you—and that will bring blessings upon your family.

> *Lord, my kids need a better dad. Make me that dad, I pray. Forgive me, free me from anything that would hold me back, and help me follow You, the best Dad of all. Amen.*

Your Spiritual Heritage

Here's an understatement: Parenting is one of the hardest responsibilities in life. If you are a dad, you will understand what I'm saying. Being a parent can be downright tough at times. But if you hang in there with God, and you do your part in raising your children His way, and you resist caving in to the pressures of society (and even your own kids), you are likely to experience the incredible joy that come from seeing your kids follow after God.

As the apostle John said, "I have no greater joy than to hear that my children walk in truth" (3 John 4). While John was talking about spiritual children in that passage, we can know that same kind of joy when our birth children walk in truth as well!

God, sometimes I wonder if this is more respon-
sibility than I can handle. But You can do amaz-
ing things in my kids' lives—even through an
imperfect dad like me. Save them, O God! Amen.

Do They Know You Care?

It's funny what children will remember from their childhood. When you quiz them about the past, they might not recall the things you thought were so special, such as birthdays or certain gifts you gave to them. Rather, they're more likely to remember the special traditions you established in your family, such as your annual backpacking trip with the boys, or those monthly "date nights" with your girls.

When you develop such traditions, you show your children you care about them and want to spend time with them. That, in turn, creates an environment in which they feel comfortable sharing their hearts with you. The result? You grow closer together as family. All you have to do is give them your time…and of course, a listening ear.

Lord, help me to "be there" for my kids, to establish traditions that help them feel safe and loved. And help me make the most of every opportunity to show them I care. Amen.

Honoring Your Parents

How much thought do you give to honoring your parents? God promises that if you respect them, He will bless you: "Honor your father and your mother, that your days may be long upon the land" (Exodus 20:12).

I believe that once you marry, this promise applies to both sets of parents—yours and your wife's. Now I must quickly add that you should honor your parents for the Lord's sake, not just to receive some personal benefit. But it's nice to have God's special blessings as a result of your obedience. Do you desire that for your life and marriage? Well, the promise "that it may be well with you and you may live long on the earth" (Ephesians 6:3) is yours—*if* you will honor your parents.

God, I know my parents sacrificed for me. Help me to rise to the occasion when the time comes for me to sacrifice for them. May my words and my actions honor them. Amen.

Honor
Through Humility

Moses was one of the greatest leaders in all the Bible, and yet he is also an excellent example of humility. He worked for Jethro, his father-in-law, as a shepherd for 40 years. Then God met Moses at the burning bush and called him back to Egypt (Exodus 3:1-10). When Moses approached his father-in-law about leaving his job, he did so with humility: "Please let me go and return to my brethren who are in Egypt" (Exodus 4:18). Even though Moses had a divine call from God and was 80 years old, he didn't *tell* Jethro of his intentions to leave. Rather, he *asked* permission. This is what it means to honor your parents and in-laws—to treat them with humility. Sometimes that's hard to do, but with God's grace, it is possible.

> *Lord, even though I don't live under my parents' roof, help me to show them the respect they deserve. Guard my tongue, I pray, and help me to speak only words that build them up. Amen.*

Showing You Care

How are you doing at fulfilling the fifth commandment, which charges you to "honor your father and your mother" (Exodus 20:12)? This command isn't merely a suggestion; it's a mandate straight from God. How can you show honor to your parents and in-laws?

One way is to show real interest in what's going on in their lives. Do you personally call or write? Do you think about and pray for them? When you take time to communicate, you show that you care. And by staying in touch, you'll know how you can pray on their behalf.

Perhaps you don't live near your parents and in-laws. While distance may separate you, communication will unite you. So make an effort to show honor by reaching out, and you'll experience God's promised blessings.

> *God, do my parents know that I really do care about them? Have I demonstrated my love for them? Show me the way as I resolve to give them the honor they deserve. Amen.*

A Source of
Wise Counsel

One way you can honor your parents is by asking
for and listening to their advice. Whether they are
Christians or not, they have a perspective—based on
experience—that can be helpful. Again, Moses is an
example. When he worked as a judge for the Jewish people and listened all day long to their cases,
his father-in-law, Jethro, observed, "Both you and
these people...will surely wear yourselves out. For
this thing is too much for you; you are not able to
perform it by yourself" (Exodus 18:17-19). How did
Moses respond? He "heeded the voice of his father-
in-law" (verse 24). He wasn't too proud to take advice.
Moses delegated some of his responsibilities to others, and things became much better—all because he
was willing to listen.

> *Lord, I'm the first to admit that sometimes I'm
> too proud to accept my parents' advice. I repent,
> Lord, and I choose to take my parents' perspec-
> tive into consideration when I make big deci-
> sions. Amen.*

Nurturing Family Bonds

Sometimes relationships with parents and in-laws aren't all that ideal. The family bonds are strained for one reason or another, and we use that as an excuse to not interact with them. Another excuse we'll use is geographical distance. But with so many ways of staying in touch electronically, this really isn't a good excuse. Then there's busyness. We might say, "Oh, they'll understand. We have so much to do. They know we love them." Yet another impediment is plain selfishness. We take time to do what *we* want to do, and don't carve out time for others. But no matter what your excuse, God calls you to honor your parents. If your desire is to please Him, you will respect your parents on both sides and extend His love to them.

> *God, help me to move past my excuses and reach out to my folks. I know You will give me what I need—patience, understanding, and compassion—as I obey You in this way. Amen.*

Extending Love
Even When It's Hard

It's sad that many family relationships are not what God desires them to be. Relatives do things that hurt one another, causing anger, distrust, or separation. Don't be one who contributes to that! While you cannot change other people's hearts toward you, you can surely change yours toward them. "If it is possible, as much as depends on you, live peaceably with all men" (Romans 12:18).

So no matter what hinders family relationships, you can be the mature one who chooses to reach out and have a heart of forgiveness. And you can draw upon the resources of prayer, the Bible, and the power of the fruit of the Holy Spirit (Galatians 5:22-23) as you do so. By God's grace, you can extend love to your family.

Lord, thank You for empowering me to forgive (or ask for forgiveness), to encourage, and to love. You can break down the walls between my family members, and I trust You to do just that. Amen.

God's Will
in the Workplace

Over the years, men have often asked me how they could "know" God's will for their career. They thought if they had the answer, they would get a much clearer perspective on their jobs and their direction in life.

I tell them God's will regarding their work isn't some mystical revelation they have to hunt for. Rather, it's spelled out clearly in the Bible: "Whatever you do, do it heartily, as to the Lord and not to men" (Colossians 3:23), and "Be obedient to those who are your masters...not...as men-pleasers, but as bondservants of Christ" (Ephesians 6:5-6). When you see this as God's will for your job, it'll transform your attitude in the workplace—and have an incredibly positive impact on everyone around you!

God, it's great to know that by seeking You and retaining this mind-set, I can be confident that I'm in Your will. I choose to work heartily and honor my "masters"—because I honor You. Amen.

A Real Sense
of Purpose

Just the awareness that you're working for God should be enough to keep you motivated on the job. But there are other reasons that can motivate you: Your job helps you provide for your family. It allows you to develop a servant's heart. It is your God-given place to proclaim Christ to a watching world. And it's the calling God has given you at this time in your life.

Every one of those reasons should give you a strong sense of purpose for where you are right now in your career. When you view your job with those things in mind, you'll find work a lot more exciting. And you'll make it possible for God to use you in even greater ways than ever before.

Lord, when my job feels meaningless to me, help me to remember these encouraging truths. Thank You for the privilege of promoting Your kingdom by being a faithful worker! Amen.

Letting God Use You

Many people are dissatisfied with their jobs, and they think the grass looks greener on the other side of the fence. What causes such discontent? One is a lack of purpose. They don't see their workplace as God's calling for their life. Another is a lack of understanding. They assume work will give their life meaning when it's actually service to God, family, and co-workers that does that. Yet another is disobedience. They see work as a means to pursue worldly success and possessions.

Commit to having a positive attitude at work and thanking God for where He has placed you. For when you are content, you'll work in harmony with God's plan for you—which will make you a much better worker.

God, wherever I work, You lead me, You give my life meaning, and You provide everything I need. In You, I have it all—right where I am. Help me to glorify You at work today. Amen.

A Right
Balance

Probably the greatest battle for every working man is striking the right balance between work and family life. God wants a husband and father to provide for his family and do his best on the job. But at the same time, God does not want him to work so much he neglects his family.

This calls for balance. Have you asked God to give you wisdom about this? Can you truly say you are giving your employer a fair day's work for a fair day's pay? And can you honestly evaluate whether your job is causing you to sacrifice on family relationships? What would other people say, including your wife and children? Have the courage to make necessary changes. When you make the right choices, God will bless you.

Lord, thank You for my job and my family. They are gifts from You and important parts of Your calling on my life. Show me how to give myself to both in a balanced way. Amen.

Excelling for
the Lord's Sake

When you do your job well, you bring glory to God. So hard work is a good thing. But today's culture has different ideas about work. Many people either want everything given to them without working for it, or they don't want to work very hard to get it. You, however, as a man after God's own heart, are different. You understand God's purposes and priorities for your life. You excel at work for God and His glory, and not for men. As a result, you'll reap blessings—from knowing you are doing God's will, from knowing your wife and family benefit from your provision, and from knowing you're giving your best in the task God has entrusted to you. These blessings and more will be yours when you tend to your career God's way.

God, help me to be a worker who brings glory to You. When I am tired, may I have the satisfaction of knowing I've given my best and You will take care of the rest. Amen.

A Joyful Worker

If you have a job, you have much to be grateful for! It pays the bills and meets at least your needs, if not your wants. And it may even be a job you enjoy. Plus, if you are constantly learning about your vocation and how to get better at it, you should always be excited and growing in your work.

Above all, God is your boss (Colossians 3:22-24). Your workplace has enough complainers and whiners who are discontent and often influence others to be as miserable as they are. So be joyful. It will set you apart and give you an opportunity to share Christ when people want to know why you are so positive.

Lord, You are my ultimate source of joy, content-ment, and purpose. My job may not provide those things, but I can still be fulfilled in You and be excited about serving as an exemplary employee. Amen.

Making It Happen

Procrastination makes an unpleasant task even more painful. The longer you put it off, the more you'll have to deal with the negative consequences of not getting the job done.

Ask yourself: Why am I putting a project off? Does it seem too overwhelming? Then break it into smaller parts and do them one at a time. Are you delaying because you don't know where to begin? Swallow your pride and ask for advice. Whatever the holdup, find a way to begin moving forward. Get started...now! Once you've taken those first steps you'll gain momentum, and you'll find it easier to continue until you're finished. Then you'll know the good feeling of having that project behind you.

God, am I stuck in a project at home or at work? Have I let others down by not following through? Show me where to invest my attention and how to move forward. Thank You. Amen.

Taking Breaks

As I said earlier, marriage is hard work. Elizabeth and I have been married 40-plus years, and we still have to work daily on our relationship. Because we labor at home as writers dealing with a lot of material and constant deadlines, things can get pretty serious. So at times we just stop...and go for a walk in the woods, or go to the lake. Then if we really want to have fun, we go find a bookstore and browse for hours. More often than not, we make no purchases. You see, the fun is in being together—that's the whole purpose of breaking away.

Have you had any fun with your wife lately? What does she enjoy doing alone with you? Make time for it to happen—soon!

Lord, thank You for reminding me that it's okay to "waste" a little time by enjoying life with my wife. I pray for creativity as I think of ways to enjoy time alone with her. Amen.

Keeping Marital Joy Alive

When you walk in the Spirit you'll experience joy, which is among the fruit of the Spirit (Galatians 5:22). You'll know joy over your salvation, the joy of eternal life, and the joy that the Lord is your strength (Nehemiah 8:10). But what about marital joy—the kind that comes from a lifelong relationship with your wife? Proverbs 5:18-19 says to husbands: "Rejoice with the wife of your youth...always be enraptured with her love." When you first became married to your beloved, you were thrilled to be together, right? So don't let the burdens of life cause you to drift apart. Make time to relive the joy you knew when you started dating. It'll bring you closer together, and bring fun into your marriage as well!

God, save us from settling into a boring and lifeless marriage. Thank You for the promise of joy! Help us to remember that You can renew us—individually and as a couple—day by day. Amen.

Delighting in Your Wife

The Bible repeatedly speaks of the sexual relationship between a husband and wife in a way that suggests they should enjoy physical intimacy with each other. For example, in the book the Song of Solomon we note Solomon's desire to whisk away his bride: "Rise up, my love, my fair one, and come away!" (2:13). And we sense anticipation in her response: "Come, my beloved, let us go forth to the field...let us see if the vine has budded, whether the grape blossoms are open, and the pomegranates are in bloom. There I will give you my love" (7:11-12).

When you take time to nurture sexual intimacy with your wife, you'll enjoy that kind of desire and anticipation for each other as well.

Lord, thank You for including the Song of Solomon in the Bible! Help my wife and me to experience ever-increasing desire and delight in our physical relationship. Amen.

Casting Your Burdens
upon God

It's easy to let the cares of the world diminish the fun and joy you knew in the early years of marriage. These cares might include the press of limited finances, the pull of both of you working, the responsibilities of caring for children, the pressures of building a career, the problem of falling into a routine, or the predicament of poor health.

While you cannot ignore these cares, you can certainly yield them up to the Lord. Don't let life's pressures rob you of the joys of marriage. As 1 Peter 5:7 says, "Cast all your anxiety on him because he cares for you" (NIV). Letting God carry your burdens will free you to enjoy your marriage no matter what your circumstances.

> *God, help me to trust You with the concerns on my heart today. May I know the joy of trusting You, and may that joy infect everyone in my household. Amen.*

Serving Together

The most rewarding fun you can have in a marriage is serving the Lord together. That's because it has eternal value and blesses others along the way.

This can take shape in many forms. You can teach a class together. You can go to Christian camps and serve as volunteer workers. You can do behind-the-scenes jobs at church, such as setting up for class, getting refreshments ready, helping clean up after an activity, joining a prayer group, visiting the hospital or shut-ins, or writing letters and preparing care packages for missionaries or Third-World children.

This will definitely make a difference in your marriage—there's something about serving God as a couple that keeps you focused on Him and draws you closer together.

Lord, forgive me for focusing so much on my own little world. Open my eyes to see the needs around me and the gifts You have given my wife and me to meet those needs. Amen.

Focusing on Your Family

When it comes to making time for your wife and kids, how about turning off the television for a night?

Before televisions were invented, families spent their evenings talking, planning trips and holidays, reading, and playing games together. The television has snatched all that away and substituted the warmth of personal involvement and fun with impersonal entertainment.

Set aside one night a week and use it to have fun with each other as a couple or with your family—without the distraction of television. The adjustment might be a bit hard at first, but in time, these evenings will become a cherished family tradition.

God, an evening with no TV would be great, but taking that first step can be tough. I ask for wisdom and creativity so I can facilitate enjoyable interactions with my family. Amen.

Spontaneity

Back when you first got married, your universe was made up of just the two of you, so you were able to spend a lot of time just having fun together. It's probably a lot harder now to break away from the distractions of work and home, but doing so will do wonders for your marriage. Ask your wife what she would like to do for recreation on an evening or weekend. She may suggest some activities you wouldn't consider fun, but be ready for some give-and-take. You go to the mall with her, and she goes to the ballpark with you. That's fair, isn't it? Keep in mind that whatever she suggests is important to her, and if that's the case, it should also be important to you!

Lord, when our daily routines start to strangle the life out of our marriage, please help us breathe in the fresh air of spontaneity, relaxation, and fun. Help us enjoy our lives—and each other! Amen.

Saved to Serve

Bud Wilkinson, the legendary coach of the University of Oklahoma football team from 1947 to 1963, once described the game of football as "50,000 people who desperately need exercise watching 22 men who desperately need rest." Unfortunately that is the situation in most churches today. Spiritually gifted believers are sitting in the pews watching a small handful of others do all the serving.

As Christians, we are saved to serve. Ephesians 2:10 says, "We are [the Lord's] workmanship, created in Christ Jesus for good works." A believer who isn't serving is like a car that's been put on blocks. That makes the car useless! Are you serving? God brought you into the church for the purpose of rendering useful and beneficial service.

God, I don't want to be in the bleachers when You are calling me to be on the field. Help me find my position on Your team and fill it with the strength You provide. Amen.

A Living Sacrifice

Service that counts is service that costs. Think about it: We usually place less value on things that are given to us than on things we have paid for. The only difference in the Christian life is that our salvation didn't cost us anything. Rather, it cost God everything. He sent His only Son to the cross to pay the very high price for redeeming us from sin.

Shouldn't that make you and me willing to sacrifice ourselves for the sake of Christ's body, the church? He gave His life for us…and we ought to give our lives for Him in return. Paul put it this way: "Present your bodies a living sacrifice, holy, acceptable to God, which is your *reasonable service*" (Romans 12:1).

Lord, I pray for a new perspective today. When I sacrifice my time or money or energy, help me to see how small those sacrifices really are compared to Your great sacrifice for the world. Amen.

Steps to Serving

If you are already actively serving God and His people, that's great. Keep it up! But if not, the question you should ask is, "How can I begin to serve?"

First, *be informed*. Read your Bible to get a better understanding of what spiritual gifts are and how they work. Start by reading 1 Corinthians 12 and Romans 12:3-8. Find out all you can about these "abilities." Second, *be willing*. This is the hardest part about getting started. God is not going to force you to serve Him. No, doing that is your choice. So what will you do? That brings up the last step—*be available*. Find an opportunity and sign up. And as you serve, you'll bring honor to God and blessings to others.

> God, please lead me as I step out into a new area of service. And help me capitalize on small opportunities to humbly serve people all around me in my everyday life. Amen.

Faithful in the Small Things

My service in the church began with washing pots and pans at socials and showing up for "workdays" on Saturday morning, during which we would do maintenance work around the property. As I grew spiritually, I was given other responsibilities. And as I was faithful, God moved me into greater areas of service. It all started with a willingness to serve, and God did the rest.

And the most exciting part? My wife, Elizabeth, got involved as well. As we both served, we grew spiritually—which brought greater blessings and fulfillment to our marriage. Yes, service will require personal sacrifice on your part. But the spiritual dividends you'll reap are well worthwhile.

Lord, thank You for opportunities to say no to pride and yes to humble service. Throughout each day, please remind me that faithful service in the small things will lead to greater responsibilities. Amen.

A Team
Impact

Have you met Priscilla and Aquila? This couple is mentioned in three different chapters of the Bible. They were gracious, hospitable, and helped the apostle Paul further the cause of Christ in new places. And they were fearless—there was widespread persecution of Christians by the Roman government in the early church, yet they trusted God and served in spite of danger. As a result Paul commended them, saying, "Greet Priscilla and Aquila, my fellow workers...who risked their own necks for my life, to whom not only I give thanks, but also all the churches of the Gentiles" (Romans 16:3-4). Paul's praise confirms the great impact a couple can have as they serve God together!

> *God, could my wife and I possibly have a substantial impact on other people's lives? Could we really know the joy of serving together in meaningful ways? I'm ready—lead us, Father. Amen.*

Expanding
Your Horizons

Serving as a husband-wife team is a great way to increase your effectiveness to the body of Christ. Each of you brings special gifts, abilities, and experiences that can help others. And whether you serve separately or together, not only are you building up others, but you are also contributing to your own spiritual growth.

Every once in a while, opportunities will come along that allow you to crank up your service a notch. How about in place of your next vacation you take a short-term missions trip? That's sacrificial service... and an adventure to boot! Service in the church has its rewards, and serving together on the mission field will take you to a whole new level. You'll find it a life-changing experience.

> *Lord, I confess that I think too small when it comes to service. Help my wife and me to step out, to think more broadly, and to trust You to do great things through us. Amen.*

Little Things,
Big Difference

What's great about serving God is that there are many "little things" you can do to help other believers or the church, even if you don't have any training. It may seem a little thing to sweep the floors, pick up after the Sunday service, help with repairs around the building, set up chairs. But those little things are what make the big things go smoothly and contribute to making church a better experience for all. It's remarkable how that which may seem insignificant really does make a big difference.

So don't ever disdain the little things. Every bit of help counts. Every person has an important role. Maybe your work takes place behind the scenes, but God is paying attention. And He will reward you when you are faithful in the little things.

God, is my system of measurement different from Yours? Is a little act of service actually a big deal to You? Help me to see deeper meaning and greater value in "small" acts of service. Amen.

Spreading
the Enthusiasm

Do you know a couple who faithfully serve the Lord? A couple you really enjoy being around? What do you appreciate most about them?

My hope is that you and your wife know one or two couples in your church that you look up to as role models. I think you know what kind of people I mean. They are always building up others. You look forward to your every interaction with them. In time, as you learn and grow from their example, you too can start having that kind of influence on other couples who are younger. You can share the riches of your own blessings and pass them on to others. After all, that is the goal of service—to encourage fellow believers in the church!

Lord, thank You for our wonderful role models. Please lead my wife and me in a process of becoming inspirational role models for others, and help us take note of those who need encouragement. Amen.

Twice
the Blessing

When you and your wife join hands, hearts, and feet to take the good news about Jesus Christ to others, your service becomes a doubly rewarding experience. One of the things that draws us closer to God is sharing our faith—and doing that together would make you a couple after God's own heart.

Why is this news about Jesus so good? Because His death for our sins offers freedom—from guilt, a meaningless life, and spiritual death. That's good news! And as Paul said, "Beautiful are the feet of those who bring good news!" (Romans 10:15 NIV). Won't you and your wife commit to building the kinds of relationships with your loved ones, neighbors, and acquaintances that makes it possible to share this news with them?

God, make my family a light to people who are in darkness. May our words simply confirm what others can already tell—that You are transforming our lives and can do the same for them. Amen.

Opening the Doors

What would you do if you were a missionary in a foreign country who desired to reach out to others with the gospel of Jesus Christ? You would build relationships with the people around you so you could eventually share that message, right?

Well, guess what? You don't have to go to a foreign country to serve as a missionary and witness, and you don't have to learn another language. You are a missionary right where you are. Together with your wife, pray for your neighbors by name. Invite them into your home. And allow them to observe your marriage and family life. In these ways, you will open doors of opportunity that may allow you to share Christ with them.

Lord, please help my family notice the simple ways we can build new friendships. As we invite others into our home and lives, may they see the life-changing work You are doing in us. Amen.

The Power of Your Actions

What if you don't feel comfortable about sharing your faith with your neighbors? Well, there are many ways you can build bridges with them so that your "comfort level" is no longer an issue.

For example, you can participate in neighborhood yard sales or block parties. Volunteer to feed your neighbors' pets while they are on vacation. Pick up their mail and bring in their newspapers. Water their garden or lawn. None of these activities require you to say a word about your beliefs. But your joyful spirit and servant attitude will speak volumes about your faith. Hopefully as you give and expect nothing in return, your neighbors will want to know what makes you different. And that, in turn, will let you share with them. Who knows what God will do in their hearts?

God, help my family to pay attention to others, to serve them, to pray for them, and to shine Your light in our neighborhood. Amen.

Who Can You Invite?

Your local church is God's gift to you and your family, and it is also God's gift to a lost world. Just as your family is blessed by the programs offered at your church, your neighbors and workmates can receive a blessing from them as well.

Don't be shy—be excited about what's going on there. Share that enthusiasm with others. They need the saving hand of Jesus, and your church is just the place where they might meet Him. Invite the neighborhood children to youth activities. Invite their parents to seminars on parenting and marriage. Take them with you to a family or couples' retreat. You do the praying and inviting, and let God take it from there.

Lord, thank You for my church. It's not perfect, but You have called us together to fellowship, worship, learn, pray, and serve. Who can I invite to church today? Amen.

Embracing Your Role

Many Christian men tend to delegate the spiritual education of the children to their wife. But that's not God's design for you as a man. Ephesians 6:4 is clear about your responsibility to your kids: "Fathers… bring them up in the training and admonition of the Lord."

I know you are busy and you have many things competing for your time and attention. But don't expect your children to embrace your faith and make it their own until they have witnessed the strength of your relationship with God. Let them see you live out the Christian life. The only way that can happen is to give them long, sustained looks at what a believer looks like. And that, of course, means spending time together with them.

God, help me live my faith out in the open for all to see. Whether I'm reading, praying, serving, making decisions, or just talking or playing, may my kids see You in my life. Amen.

Compassion
on Display

Some people think compassion is not a very "manly" emotion. But is that trait to be exhibited only by women? You know the answer, don't you? Jesus is the perfect example of a man who demonstrated this emotion. He sorrowed over people's unbelief (Luke 19:41). He wept for His friend Lazarus (John 11:35). When He saw people in need, "He was moved with compassion" (Matthew 9:36).

When was the last time you wept for the salvation of someone, or for a person who was deeply hurting? If compassion is not one of your strengths (and it should be, as you follow Christ's example), then pray and ask God to soften your heart so this quality is on display in your life.

Jesus, thank You for being an example of a compassionate man. I pray that my family, friends, and co-workers would all know that I care for them and that I'm moved by their concerns. Amen.

Letting God Do His Work

Every man hopes to have an impact on his world. But influence is costly, for it demands hard work. It takes time to build, and it involves helping other people. It is hard-won and easily lost. It takes responsibility, and it calls for sensitivity in your relationships with others. But that shouldn't discourage you. The good news is that, with God's help, influence is attainable by anyone.

When you look at the men in the Bible who had the greatest impact on others, you'll notice they all shared a key trait: They yielded their lives fully to God. They submitted their all to Him. As a result, God was free to work powerfully through them. And you can let God do the same through you.

Lord, I choose to seek You and obey You today. As You work in my life, I trust that You will help me share simple words and acts of service so people are drawn to You. Amen.

Ordinary Person, Extraordinary God

The apostle Paul is a prime example of someone who had great influence. He spread the gospel far and wide, and wrote much of the New Testament. Have you noticed the qualities that set him apart are within your reach? He was obedient, he served others, he was humble, he prayed, he trusted God, he was empowered by the Spirit, he loved and read the Scriptures, and he was faithful in the tasks God gave him. In every way he was an ordinary person empowered by an extraordinary God.

You too can have great influence. It takes a willingness to do the basics God asks of every believer. And the best part is, you do it all in God's power. Isn't that amazing?

God, as I seek You and humbly serve others today, may Your relationship with me grow deeper and Your influence through me grow broader. Thank You. Amen.

It's Never Too Late

Paul was an amazingly influential believer—and yet did you know he got a late start in the Christian life? Most people become Christians as teens and young adults; Paul didn't get started in formal ministry until he was past 40. Most pastoral search committees would never consider a man in his mid-forties with little to no experience! And remember—back in those days, someone that age was pretty old.

In spite of his late start, Paul had a great impact. This teaches us two important lessons: (1) It's never too late to start serving God, and (2) it's never too late to change the course of your life so you can make a difference. No matter what your age or circumstance, God can always use you.

> *Lord, help me believe that You can influence other people for good through me. Today I turn away from my excuses for holding back, and I choose to serve the people You bring my way. Amen.*

Staying
the Course

When hardships come, many Christians feel like checking out. When life goes wrong, when finances get worse, when a job becomes difficult, or family life falls apart, they say, "I've had it. I quit. I don't see God helping me. I'm just not cut out for the Christian life."

If that ever happens to you, remember this: God can work through adversity. And He is with you at all times when life gets rough. Consider Paul—he was persecuted, beaten, jailed, and threatened with death. But he didn't falter. He waited on God and trusted Him. And he said, "I can do all things through Christ who strengthens me" (Philippians 4:13). From Paul you learn that hardship can be the training ground for a life of impact.

> *God, I don't enjoy hardships. But if they come with the package of serving You, and if You can use them to make me a better man, then I'll stay the course and follow You. Amen.*

All Things
Are Possible

Maybe you've wondered if God can really use you. You don't have much training, you're getting a late start in life, or adversity has held you back a lot. Or maybe it's something as simple as the fact you're a relatively new believer and you don't know your Bible well yet.

If so, you're in good company. In the Bible you find many people who found themselves in similar predicaments—yet God worked mightily through them. This affirms an important truth: "With God all things are possible" (Matthew 19:26).

All that to say, don't ever let a supposed lack of qualifications or seemingly prohibitive circumstances get you down. God is able…and He will enable you.

> *Lord, I'm not qualified to play much of a part in Your kingdom. But You do incredible things through underdogs, so today I'll focus less on my weakness and more on Your strength. Amen.*

In Control
of the Future

Life is full of surprises. You never know when things may take a sudden and unexpected turn for the worse. And when they do, you may find yourself saying, "What happened?"

You can take comfort in the fact God is never caught by surprise. He is in control of the future, and He will never allow you into a situation beyond your ability to handle. That doesn't mean He will make life easier for you—just that He will sustain you and enable you to persevere. As God said to Paul, "My grace is sufficient for you, for My strength is made perfect in weakness" (2 Corinthians 12:9). When you trust God in your weakness, His grace will hold you and shine forth.

God, I don't know what's going to happen, but You know every potential outcome. I don't adapt or execute very well, but You can do anything. Thank You for pouring Your strength into me today. Amen.

Simple Trust

When things go wrong, we usually ask, "God, why did that happen?" But if you read the Bible carefully, you'll notice an interesting pattern: God never asks us to figure out the *why* behind our circumstances. Instead, He simply asks us to *trust* Him: "Trust in the Lord with all your heart, and lean not on your own understanding" (Proverbs 3:5).

Are you able to say with Paul, "Oh, the depth of the riches both of the wisdom and knowledge of God! How unsearchable are His judgments and His ways past finding out!" (Romans 11:33)? That's what it means to trust God—to place complete confidence in Him and rest in the knowledge He will take care of you, even when you don't understand what's going on.

Lord, I'm not able to figure out why some things happen. But I am able to trust You, so that's what I'll focus on today. Help me to be confident in You in every situation. Amen.

Never
Forget

If you've been a Christian any length of time, you know how easy it is to forget the greatness of what happened at the moment of salvation. You shouldn't, for what took place at that time was an astounding miracle. You were…

- rescued from the dominion of darkness (Colossians 1:13)
- brought into the kingdom of the Son (1:13)
- forgiven of all sins (1:14)
- made spiritually alive together with Christ (Ephesians 2:5)
- given the gift of eternal life (Romans 6:23)

Won't you take a moment right now to thank God for all He has done for you?

God, what an incredible gift! What an amazing miracle! You have changed my life, and I am so thankful and amazed. As I learn more about my salvation, may I turn to You in praise. Amen.

A Great Treasure

The Bible is a truly remarkable book. And the more you know about it, the more you'll appreciate it. Consider what Psalm 19:7-11 says:

It is the perfect law (verse 7). The Bible has no errors. It is historically accurate and provides spiritual truth.

It is a rule book for daily living (verse 8). Scripture is always 100 percent right. You can trust what it says about how to live.

It is eternal (verse 9). Other books come and go, but the Bible endures forever.

It is a treasure (verse 10). It contains everything you need for life and godliness (2 Peter 1:3). Nothing else can do that.

> *Father, thank You for reminding me today that the Bible is an incredible treasure. Open my ears and eyes so I can receive Your truth and respond accordingly. Amen.*

A Help at
All Times

What are some ways the Bible helps you? Again, look at what Psalm 19:7-11 says:

It refreshes and heals. The Bible converts the sinner and restores the believer who stumbles (verse 7).

It gladdens the heart. Scripture is a source of true joy (verse 8).

It illuminates the mind. The Bible gives meaning to life (verse 8).

It satisfies. As food satisfies the body, Scripture satisfies the soul (verse 10).

It rewards. There is no greater reward than a clean conscience, a pure heart, and peace of mind. All this comes not just from *knowing* God's Word, but *keeping* it (verse 11).

> *Lord, I pray that every time the culture around me suggests a path to happiness, You will remind me that true and lasting satisfaction comes through knowing You in Your Word. Amen.*

From God Himself

What is it that makes the Bible so special?

Unlike all the other books in the world, it's written by God, who alone possesses perfect knowledge and wisdom. It has a divine origin. Second Timothy 3:16 says, "All Scripture is given by inspiration of God." The term "inspiration" here means "God-breathed"—the Bible is filled with the breath of God, and it is the Spirit who enabled men of God to write the Word of God (2 Peter 1:21).

No other book can make that claim. Are you giving the Bible the place it deserves in your life? Where is there room for improvement, and how can you make that happen?

> *God, You are actually talking to me through the Bible! I admit I don't always pay attention. Forgive me, I pray, and guide me as I consider practical ways to take in Your Word. Amen.*

Two Key Purposes

While the Bible is a big book, ultimately it has two purposes, according to 2 Timothy 3:15-17:

Salvation—God's Word alone is "able to make you wise for salvation through faith which is in Christ Jesus" (verse 15).

Sanctification—Once we're saved, we're called to grow. That happens when we read, study, and obey the Bible, which profits us in these ways: It instructs us about God and right living, it convicts us of sin, it corrects our wrong thinking, and it equips us for every good work (verses 16-17).

What most recent benefit have you enjoyed from Scripture? Take a moment to thank God for that today.

Father, thank You for what You have accomplished in me through Your Word—You give me new life, show me what You are like, guide me each day, and so much more. Amen.

Soaking in
the Word

To what extent are you allowing Scripture to do its empowering work in your life?

It's not enough to interact with the Bible on a superficial level. If you really want to know the power of God's Word, it needs to "dwell in you richly" (Colossians 3:16). That means reading it and studying it. As the apostle Paul told his disciple Timothy, "Be diligent to present yourself approved to God, a worker who does not need to be ashamed, rightly dividing the word of truth" (2 Timothy 2:15). When you let God's Word thoroughly permeate you, you'll receive the wisdom, maturity, and strength you need for living a victorious Christian life. In fact, your life will become something others want—and want to follow.

God, I pray Your Word will go deep into the core of my being. Help me cooperate with Your work in my life by giving Scripture the time, priority, and respect it deserves. Amen.

Going Against the Grain

Living according to God's Word is a tall order in today's immoral society. For that matter, it's never been easy to live for God—not in Paul's day, not in the days since the sexual revolution, nor during any other period in Christian history.

Yet God wants you to be His man—a man who has resolve to live according to Scripture. A man who cares more about pleasing God than pleasing people.

And He has given you the resources to stand strong in the face of opposition. When you respond to God and allow His Word to fill you, the Holy Spirit will empower you with the courage you need to persevere and live in obedience rather than compromise.

Lord, may this be a good day—a day of standing strong against disobedience and compromise, a day filled with Your Word and the power of the Holy Spirit. Amen.

Unlimited Potential

There's no way to adequately describe all the ways God's Word can change you. This list only scratches the surface: The Bible can equip you for every good work (2 Timothy 3:17), stimulate your spiritual growth (Acts 20:32), give you wisdom (Proverbs 4:11), give you peace (Proverbs 3:1-2), give you direction (Psalm 119:105), keep you from sin (Psalm 119:11), give you power (Colossians 1:11), and give you discernment for godly living (Hebrews 5:14).

Notice I didn't say, "The Bible *will...*" I said, "The Bible *can...*" All the power and potential you need for change and growth is available—when you look to God's Word, learn God's Word, and keep God's Word.

Father, thank You for giving me all I need to become more like You. Today I choose to do my part—to take in Your Word and follow it as You empower me. Amen.

The Blessing
of Confession

Unconfessed sin always hinders your progress toward spiritual maturity. So to ensure that your growth remains steady and uninterrupted, keep a short record of sins with God. Confess any and all sins to Him right away. If you want to experience a close, ongoing relationship with Him, do as David did in Psalm 32 and admit your sins, whether big or small. There, David confessed his affair with Bathsheba and his subsequent murder of her husband (2 Samuel 11). Make confession a habit so you can experience the wonderful cleansing that comes afterward.

David wrote in Psalm 32:1, "Blessed is he whose transgression is forgiven, whose sin is covered." Don't try to hide your sin—lift it upward to God and ask for His forgiveness. Then you'll know blessing and growth.

God, You know everything about me...and love me anyway! Thank You in advance for forgiving me and healing me as I talk with You about my failures. Amen.

Day
by Day

When the people of Israel wandered in the wilderness for 40 years, God provided food for them, which they had to gather daily. The manna never lasted beyond the day it was given, and in the same way they had to obtain their physical food every day, you should pursue your spiritual food every day. When it comes to maturity, you cannot rest or count on yesterday's growth. You may think you can get by for a while without reading your Bible, praying, and remaining accountable to God. But without ongoing spiritual nourishment, you'll wake up one day and find yourself weak and defeated.

Don't try to slide by on yesterday's growth. Dedicate yourself daily to spiritual nourishment. *That* will make you a man after God's own heart.

Lord, I believe You have more for me—more ways I can be like You and more opportunities to share Your blessings with others. Today and every day I need new life from You. Amen.

Persevering in Prayer

Prayer is a spiritual discipline that is difficult for even the most devout Christian to practice on a truly consistent basis. It demands time and requires focus, which are hard for modern minds and lifestyles to accommodate. To pray in dependence upon God also requires us to overcome our natural tendency to try to come up with our own solutions to life's problems. Prayer tries our patience. We dislike waiting on God for His answers. So we try to manipulate our situation by coming up with our own quick answers.

Don't let the struggle to pray discourage you. Ask God to keep you from being distracted by the world around you, to give you a God-focus, and to help you wait patiently for His answers. That will help you to persevere in this vital area of your Christian life.

Father, sometimes I feel like a child who is just learning to talk to his dad. Thank You for being even more excited about my faltering attempts than that dad is about his son's first words. Amen.

Praying
with Confidence

When you pray to God, you are talking to someone you can't see, someone whose existence is tangibly validated only by what you see of His handiwork in creation (Romans 1:20) or by the revelation of Himself in the Bible. So prayer is the purest form of faith, which is described as "the substance of things hoped for, the evidence of things not seen" (Hebrews 11:1). Yet the faith of prayer is not based on vivid imagination or wishful thinking. It is based on the promises of God, which are found in the Bible.

Scripture says, "There has not failed one word of all His good promise" (1 Kings 8:56). God has a perfect track record when it comes to keeping His promises. Therefore you can pray with confidence that God will fulfill every single one.

God, talking with someone I can't see isn't always easy. But I can see what You have revealed about Yourself in the Bible, and that's enough for me to have confidence in You. Amen.

Waiting for God's Answers

When you think your prayers aren't being answered, you tend to get discouraged and cry out, "God, why aren't You helping me?"

Yet God has promised to answer your prayers: "Ask, and it will be given to you; seek, and you will find; knock, and it will be opened to you" (Matthew 7:7). However, sometimes you don't see the answer for a while, or God may say no because He has a different—and better—plan.

So you are exhorted to ask. But your request must be...

- in faith (Matthew 21:22),

- without selfish motives (James 4:3), and

- according to the will of God (1 John 5:14-15).

Lord, I confess that I'm not good at waiting for Your answers to my prayers. But as I wait, I believe You will build my faith, purify my heart, and show me Your will. Thank You!

Always Ready to Listen

When you fail to pray, you end up feeling distant from God. And that, in turn, makes upi even more reluctant to pray.

No matter how distant you might feel from the Lord, God is always close by. He hasn't changed, moved, disappeared, or lost interest in you. So close the gap. Take a simple step toward God and talk to Him. The more you do this, the more comfortable you'll become communicating with Him. And the more you pray, the more opportunity you'll have to ask for His help for yourself and on behalf of others. And the more you ask, the more answers and guidance you'll receive. No matter what your situation, God is always ready to listen!

Father, thank You for always being near, always listening, and always caring. Help me to look to You in every situation and to never allow a gap to develop between us. Amen.

Too Busy to Pray?

Often when you fail to pray, you say it's because you're so busy. But in reality, it's not your schedule that keeps you from praying. It's your failure to realize the importance of prayer and *make* the time to pray.

And instead of relying upon the power of prayer in all that you do, you turn to your feeble wisdom and energy. You roll up your sleeves and get busy, turning to your own power instead of God's.

If your life is so busy you can't pray, have you ever considered it's because you haven't taken time to ask God for help with your priorities? Turn to Him, and He will give you the discernment that enables you to use your time well so that you are able to pray.

> *God, show me—what have I prioritized above my time with You? What have I depended on instead of You? Help me assess my priorities today and keep prayer at the top of the list. Amen.*

When You Need Wisdom

Are you experiencing a difficult problem in your life right now? Are you at a crossroad with regard to a major decision? Are you struggling with issues you don't have answers for? If yes, hear this promise from your heavenly Father: "If any of you lacks wisdom, let him ask of God, who gives to all liberally and without reproach, and it will be given to him" (James 1:5).

God stands ready to give you wisdom. Remember, He is the source of it: "Oh, the depth of the riches both of the wisdom and knowledge of God!" (Romans 11:33). And when you don't understand what is happening, you need to wait, trust Him, and rest in His care. He is always faithful to His own.

Lord, I'll be the first to admit it—I need Your wisdom! Help me to wait on You and to put into practice the things You show me in Your Word. Amen.

Saying Yes to God

God is able to use a man who is willing to do whatever He says. By this I mean a person who listens to and obeys Him.

We see confirmation of this in the Bible. For example, the apostle Paul was asked to *get up*—and spread the gospel. Abraham was asked to *give up*—to sacrifice his son Isaac up to God, until God spared Isaac. Moses was asked to *speak up*—to confront Pharaoh about letting the people of Israel go. And Daniel was asked to *stand up*—to not yield to demands to compromise his faith. In every case, God rewarded the obedience these men showed.

When you yield yourself in complete and whole-hearted obedience to God, He can do great things through you.

> *Father, show me how I can honor You in every-thing I do at home, at work, and when I'm just having fun. I choose in advance to say yes to You in all I do! Amen.*

The Power of Obedience

When you consider the extraordinary ways God worked through men such as Moses and Paul, you may think, *I can't measure up to people like them. I don't have what they had.*

But you must realize that these "heroes" of the faith were just common, ordinary people. It was their obedience—their complete yieldedness to God—that gave them uncommon strength and faith. They submitted their lives to God, which freed God to work through them.

I don't know about you, but their examples inspire me to re-evaluate my own obedience. Am I reluctant to listen to God because I think He is asking the impossible? Am I failing to make myself available to Him because I'm doubtful or afraid? Your part is to simply obey, and God will do His part.

God, I see now that You can do anything through me if I will simply yield myself to You. Help me to make myself more available to You today. Amen.

At the Center
of God's Will

Do you know what I believe is the icing on the cake of obedience, what I believe to be one of the most compelling reasons for choosing to obey God? It is this: Obedience leads to a powerful, confident life. When you are obedient, and when you allow yourself to be led by God through the unexpected, you then have a confidence based on the fact that you know you are exactly where God wants you to be. You won't find yourself doubting the circumstances in your life or the direction things are going. We'll have the inner peace and joy that comes from knowing you are at the center of God's will!

Lord, thank You for leading me to the center of Your will. Help me to see Your hand in everything that comes my way as I follow You today. Amen.

God-confidence

Are you fearful because God appears to be moving you in an unexpected direction? Is the unknown causing you to waver on the path of obedience? Take heart in your resolve. Walk in confidence with God. Walk as King David did, declaring, "Though I walk through the valley of the shadow of death, I will fear no evil; for You are with me" (Psalm 23:4).

Though you might not know where God's will is taking you, you can trust God to watch over and stay with you. Though life may take surprising turns, they are not unexpected to God. He knows what is happening and why, and all He calls you to do is to trust Him.

Father, I affirm that as long as You lead me and I walk with You, I have nothing to fear. I resolve to follow You today, knowing that I'm never safer than when I'm with You. Amen.

Making the Best Decisions

What if you're uncertain about an important decision you must make? How can you seek God's input? Here are the four C's you'll find helpful for the times when you need guidance:

Commands from the inspired Word of God

Competent and wise counselors

Circumstances and changing conditions

Conscience aided by the Holy Spirit

God can use any or all of these means to give direction to you if you are ready to listen. It may take time, but that's okay. Making use of these resources will help you to make informed choices that honor and glorify God.

God, I want to make wise decisions that glorify You. Help me to keep my eyes and ears open so I can learn from You and honor You in all I say and do. Amen.

Great Is His Faithfulness

How often do you take time to pause and revel in how faithful God has been to you?

Recognizing God's good help to you is important. It's when you remember His unceasing care that you are reminded He will carry you through every situation in life, no matter how bad. It was God's faithfulness in adversity that led King David to write, "I waited patiently for the LORD; and He inclined to me, and heard my cry. He also brought me up out of a horrible pit, out of the miry clay; and set my feet upon a rock, and established my steps. He has put a new song in my mouth—praise to our God; many will see it and fear, and will trust in the LORD" (Psalm 40:1-3).

Lord, You've pulled me out of a few "horrible pits" and established my steps. Help me to never forget what You have done, to always praise You, and to eagerly share Your faithfulness with others. Amen.

When It's Hard to Have Hope

When something terrible happens in your life, are you ever tempted to ask, "What good could come out of this?" It *looks* like a disaster. It *feels* like a disaster. Therefore you conclude, "It *is* a disaster!"

That's when you want to remember God's promise, "I know the thoughts that I think toward you... thoughts of peace and not of evil, to give you a future and a hope" (Jeremiah 29:11). And then there's Romans 8:28, which says, "All things work together for good to those who love God."

God doesn't tell you you'll escape suffering or pain. Rather, He promises to miraculously use even bad situations for your ultimate good, and He assures you that you have a great future ahead of you. Let these promises sustain you when you find it's hard to have hope.

> *Father, when I suffer, please strengthen me with Your Word and Your Spirit so I can endure with joy, knowing that You ultimately have great things in store for me. Amen.*

Always There
with You

Do you ever think about the fact that God knows, in advance, everything that will happen?

That means there is nothing that takes God by surprise—even the difficult crises in your life. So when you find yourself worried about tomorrow, lift your cares up to the Lord. He has already seen the future, and because He is faithful, He will give you whatever you need to persevere through your problems. In the same way that He sustained the psalmist "through the valley of the shadow of death" (Psalm 23:4), He will preserve and comfort you in every trial you face. That's why you can rejoice with David and say, "Surely goodness and mercy shall follow me all the days of my life" (verse 6).

> *God, I don't know what might happen tomorrow, but You do. I can't cause good to come from any crisis, but You can. I won't always be able to meet my own needs, but You will. Thank You.*

Restoring Hope

When worry strikes, we usually get discouraged or even depressed. We respond to life negatively, and take our eyes off God and His promises to take care of us. The next time worry strikes, here's how you can restore your hope:

Pray—"Be anxious for nothing, but in everything by prayer and supplication...let your requests be made known to God" (Philippians 3:6).

Trust—Refuse to worry about circumstances beyond your control. Remember, they are still in God's control (Psalm 135:6).

Give thanks—"In everything give thanks" (1 Thessalonians 5:18). When you thank God even for the hard things in life, you are saying, "Lord, I am confident You will use this for my good."

> *Lord, it's so easy for me to focus on the negative. Help me redeem my worried thoughts by using them as reminders to pray, to express my trust in You, and to give thanks. Amen.*

One Decision at a Time

How did men like Abraham, Daniel, and Paul become men who accomplished great things for God? There wasn't any secret formula to success for them. In fact, they were ordinary men like you and me. What made them effective leaders was their willingness to obey God, one decision at a time.

Your impact on the lives of others—your family, the people at your church, your workmates—is cultivated with each decision you make, no matter how small. It's the little things—such as reading your Bible, praying, going to church, and standing up for your faith—that add influence to your life. The key to a powerful Christian life is to obey God one decision at a time. Then He will trust you with more.

Father, may this day be filled with small steps of obedience. I pray that each choice I make today— large or small—will help me influence others for good. Amen.

Letting
God Lead

When you submit yourself to God and obey Him, you allow Him to do what He desires in your life. You make it possible for Him to lead you wherever He wants to use you.

At the same time, you'll experience the confidence that comes from knowing you are exactly where God wants you to be. You'll experience the joy of knowing you are at the center of God's will. Then you, along with Paul, can confidently lead and boldly influence others as you declare, "Imitate me, just as I also imitate Christ" (1 Corinthians 11:1).

That's why obeying God is so important. It allows Him to work through you, and it gives you a secure confidence for everyday living. Isn't that what you long for?

> *God, when I'm intimidated by a huge task before me, help me to focus on simply obeying You one step at a time. And may my life encourage others to do the same. Amen.*

Attending to
His Word

If you struggle with obeying God, ask Him to give you the strength to obey His commands. And that strength will come as you...

- faithfully read His Word,
- faithfully hear the preaching of His Word,
- faithfully listen to wise counsel from His Word, and
- faithfully deal with sin in your life as revealed by the piercing light of His Word.

Can you see how God's Word is such an important part of your life? Your willingness to obey the Lord is a key step toward experiencing God's blessings, and it will enable you to become a man God can use to make a difference.

Lord, thank You for pouring Your strength into me as I attend to Your Word. May every blessing and every trial in my life turn my obedient attention to Your Word. Amen.

Rising to the Occasion

The path of obedience is seldom easy. It certainly wasn't easy for the Christians in the New Testament era. When they preached the gospel in Jerusalem, the Jewish religious leaders told them to stop. How did they respond? They courageously declared, "Whether it is right in the sight of God to listen to you more than to God, you judge. For we cannot but speak the things which we have seen and heard" (Acts 4:19-20).

And what was the effect of their obedience? "They were all filled with the Holy Spirit, and they spoke the word of God with boldness" (verse 31). As a result, people came to Christ, and the church grew—all because they were willing to overcome challenges in their pursuit of obeying God. Are you ready to rise to the occasion?

Father, help me recognize the steps of obedience You ask me to make today. And when my commitment is challenged, help me rise to the occasion and glorify You in all I do. Amen.

Keeping Your Eye on the Prize

Because obedience has its challenges, it's the less-traveled path. Disobedience, on the other hand, is the more well-worn way. In fact, it is characterized by gridlock! Why? Because it's the easy way out. It's the road we're tempted to take when things get sticky or uncomfortable. It's the path of least resistance, and sadly, it's the path that makes us men of little or no positive impact.

As you run the race for Christ, you'll face hurdles that trip you up, knock you down, or pressure you to compromise God's standards. That's why Paul urges you to "press toward the goal for the prize of the upward call of God in Jesus Christ" (Philippians 3:14). If you keep your eye on the prize at the finish line, you'll have what it takes to overcome life's challenges.

God, instead of sneaking around the hurdles of life on the path of least resistance, I want to sail over those challenges on the high road of obedience. Please help me. Amen.

Victory over the Flesh

Every Christian man battles with the flesh—even the great apostle Paul struggled (see Romans 7:21-24). How can you M-A-S-T-E-R this challenge?

Monitor your time with those who drag you down.

Account for your struggles to a more mature believer.

Strengthen your inner man through the Bible and prayer.

Train your eyes to avoid things that stir fleshly desires.

Exercise purity in relationships with the opposite sex.

Run from the lusts of the flesh.

Victory *is* possible. Make these steps a regular part of your life!

Lord, thank You for reminding me that I am not a helpless victim. Empower me to master my fleshly desires, I pray, as I put these tools into practice. Amen.

All Ear

Have you ever tried to define *obedience*? That's the challenge a missionary ran up against as he was translating the Bible into a foreign language. Taking a break from his search for a meaning, he called to his dog. When the dog came running, a tribal observer said, "Your dog was all ear." Instantly the missionary had the words he needed to define *obedience*—"to be all ear."

How about you? Are you "all ear" when it comes to hearing what God says in His Word?

Ask the Lord to help you respond with eagerness to Scripture. You'll find this easier to do when you follow the example set by King David: "Your word I have hidden in my heart, that I might not sin against you" (Psalm 119:11).

Father, as I hide Your Word in my heart, help me to listen to its promptings and hear its life-giving message. And then, give me strength to obey—to be all ear. Amen.

Enduring Opposition

Anytime you stand up for what you believe, you will experience opposition—you can count on it! As Paul told his young disciple, Timothy, "*All* who desire to live godly in Christ Jesus will suffer persecution" (2 Timothy 3:12).

Earlier in 2 Timothy, Paul wrote, "You...must endure hardship as a good soldier of Jesus Christ. No one engaged in warfare entangles himself with the affairs of this life" (2:3-4). You are called to live boldly by different standards—God's standards.

Yes, it will be difficult. But such hardship is nothing compared to what you'll gain—God's blessing for your obedience and a clear conscience for doing what is right.

> *God, how are You asking me to stand up for what I believe today? When opposition comes my way, give me strength to bear it with grace and maintain a clear conscience. Amen.*

Tapping into God's Strength

The beauty of obedience is that what God *expects* you to do, He also *enables* you to do. The strength comes from Him. You just need a willing heart.

The apostle Paul wrote, "Be strong in the Lord and in the power of His might" (Ephesians 6:10). God has made this strength available to you, and it's pretty remarkable. Paul spoke of "the *exceeding greatness* of His power toward us who believe, according to the working of His mighty power" (Ephesians 1:19).

The power of God triumphs over all else. And you have access to it. How? Through full dependence upon Him, "praying always with all prayer and supplication in the Spirit" (6:18).

> *Lord, this is amazing. When I say yes to You—and mean it—You will give me the strength to follow through. Thank You for the "exceeding greatness" of Your power in me! Amen.*

Rejoicing in Every Victory

Growing in obedience to God is a lifelong process. It will never end. So you can expect to struggle against the desires of the flesh time and time again.

That's why it's so important to remember that spiritual growth happens one step at a time, one victory at a time. It may not seem like it at the moment, but every one of your victories—even the small ones—add up and have a cumulative effect, bringing you toward greater spiritual maturity.

So rejoice in even the smallest victories. Thank God for every time He enables you to make a right choice. And you'll find yourself inspired to persevere as new challenges come your way.

Father, help me to see the importance of every tiny step of obedience I take today. Thank You for using those steps to make me stronger, more mature, and more like You. Amen.

The Key to Focus

Have you ever felt like your life is scattered, as if you're going ten different directions? Have you wished your life was more focused?

If there's one lesson we can learn from the apostle Paul, it's the value of discipline. All his energies were passionately channeled in one direction—toward winning a "crown that will last forever" (1 Corinthians 9:25 NIV). Whereas many people chase after earthly prizes, or crowns that won't last, Paul pursued an eternal prize. He wanted to know Christ, the power of His resurrection, and the fellowship of His sufferings (Philippians 3:10). And he counted everything else but loss (3:3-7).

What is motivating you? Is Christ truly first in your life? When He is, you'll have focus.

> *God, I want to be passionate, focused, and directed. Alert me today if I start going several directions at once. Bring all my responsibilities together into a unified life of following You. Amen.*

Profitable for All Things

We live in a health-conscious society. Diet plans and exercise regiments abound, and we're reminded again and again of the benefits of eating right and good physical training.

Even the Bible acknowledges this, saying that bodily exercise "profits" us (1 Timothy 4:8). Yet notice what it says next: "But godliness is profitable for all things, having promise of the life that now is and of that which is to come." So while physical training has some value, spiritual training has a lot more. In fact, it's "profitable for *all* things." That includes your marriage, your children, your job, your ministry, and even your life in eternity!

How are you doing in your growth toward godliness—that is, becoming more like God as much as is humanly possible?

> *Lord, help me assess my spiritual training regimen and make adjustments where necessary. Thank You for the promise that my growth in godliness is not only possible but also profitable! Amen.*

The Rewards of Discipline

I'm sure you've heard the slogan "No pain, no gain." Usually we see those words posted in a gym or over a locker-room door. But these same four words are also a perfect paraphrase of the personal philosophy of the apostle Paul, who said, "I strike a blow to my body and make it my slave so that…I myself will not be disqualified for the prize" (1 Corinthians 9:27 NIV).

This kind of discipline requires effort and sacrifice. But it's well worthwhile, for you'll receive a double prize—the eternal prize Paul is talking about, and the earthly prize of accomplishment and impact. Indeed, personal discipline brings great rewards.

Father, as I focus on the prize right now, the effort, sacrifice, and pain of discipline seem much more manageable. Help me to focus on the prize all through the day today. Amen.

Imitating God

Are you a spiritually sensitive man? By way of definition, this means walking through life with a God-consciousness. It means knowing how God would act, talk, and respond to life's situations.

How can you develop this kind of sensitivity? A key way is to observe God in action in the Bible. For example, as you see how He responded graciously to His fallen creation and sacrificed His only Son for us, you begin to understand how you should be more loving, giving, and selfless. As you see His other traits—His patience, His wisdom, His goodness—you'll discover character qualities you'll want to imitate in your own life.

So observe God carefully. Learn from His example. And you'll grow in spiritual sensitivity.

God, how can I imitate You at work today? At home? In the community? Show me how my simple words and actions can reflect Your saving work in the world. Amen.

Mastering God's Word

When I was young in the Christian faith, a man came to our church to teach a seminar. It was evident that he knew his Bible very well. I admired his grasp of Scripture, and wished I had the same.

After the seminar, I summoned the courage to ask how he came to know the Bible so well. I expected him to say it was his theological training, or his ability to interpret Scripture. But to my surprise, he said it was a lifetime of just reading the Bible regularly, day in and day out.

That's pretty simple, isn't it? What a joy it was to realize every believer could have the same kind of knowledge. All it takes is faithful and consistent reading.

Lord, I pray that You would open my eyes as I read the Scriptures. May my heart be like good soil so the seed of Your Word will go deep and produce a good crop. Amen.

Godly Ambition

Ambition can be both positive and negative. An example of the latter is people who have scratched their way to the top and, in the process, left their claw marks on the backs of you and others whom they climbed over in order to reach their goal.

That's not the kind of ambition we as Christian men should have. No, we are to have a godly ambition—that is, a desire to serve the Lord and focus on fulfilling His will. God's kind of man strives solely for the glory of God and the good of others. I believe this is part of what Paul had in mind when he said, "Imitate me, just as I also imitate Christ" (1 Corinthians 11:1). Let's follow Paul's example by bringing our ambition in line with God's will.

God, when I am consumed by selfish ambition, help me focus on glorifying You and serving others. And when I lack ambition, remind me of the tremendous prize of knowing You. Amen.

The Value
of Goals

What are your goals in life? Have you defined them yet? Goals can help you in a lot of ways. For example, goals give *definition*—they take daydreams and make them concrete. Goals give *focus*—they help you know how to spend your time, and set aside time-wasters. Goals give *motivation*—they give you something to aim for, they help prod you onward when the going gets rough. Goals help you with *decision-making*—they equip you to make the best decisions about how to spend your time, money, and energy. And goals help you to have an *impact*—when you achieve them, you'll have grown as a person and hopefully others will benefit from your efforts.

So set some goals...and become the kind of man who makes a difference!

> *Lord, guide me as I assess my goals today. Help me set constructive goals, prioritize them appropriately, and submit them to Your leadership. May my goals lead to my highest goal of knowing You. Amen.*

Using Time Well

The sooner we realize that life is but a vapor (James 4:14), the more likely we are to make sure we are using our time well.

That doesn't mean you can't take time to have fun and relax. Rather, it means making sure you have your priorities in order. At the top of the list is your spiritual health. That's because it affects everything else you do. When things are right between you and God and you're spending time in His Word, that will help you align the rest of your priorities properly, which include caring for your family, managing your finances wisely, maintaining good physical health, giving your best on the job, and serving others in your church. When you've taken care of these priorities, you can be confident you are using your time well.

Father, do my priorities bring glory to You? Do they help me make the most of my short time on this earth? Help me re-evaluate my priorities and make any necessary adjustments. Amen.

A Healthy Perspective

God cares about your body and health. Scripture says that…

- your body is a *stewardship* from God
  (1 Corinthians 6:19-20)
- your body is the *temple* of the Holy Spirit
  (1 Corinthians 3:16)
- your body is meant to *glorify* God
  (1 Corinthians 6:19-20)

So how are you doing? Many people these days could eat better and use more exercise. Are you among them? Do you view your body as something that God has entrusted into your care? Having that perspective may help you to be more diligent about your physical health. And that, in turn, will help you to enjoy life more and live longer.

God, thank You for showing me this strong connection between my physical and spiritual health. How can I be a good steward of my body and glorify You with it? Lead me, Lord. Amen.

The Gift of Friends

Friends are a gift from the Lord. You should cultivate friendships with other men, especially other Christian men who will encourage you in your faith and give good advice. The Bible says, "As iron sharpens iron, so a man sharpens the countenance of his friend" (Proverbs 27:17).

Are you friends with men who are a positive influence on your life, who encourage and build you up in the faith? And are you making the effort to grow spiritually so you, in turn, can be that kind of friend to others?

If you are in need of such friends, ask God to lead you to the right people. And be willing to take time to be a friend to other men who would benefit from your wisdom and experience.

Lord, help me to build replenishing friendships with other men. Whom can I look to as an example? Whom can I encourage? Thank You for my friends! Amen.

Little Choices, Big Decisions

There are a myriad of thoughts penned on the importance of choices. You've probably heard this one:

Little choices determine habit;
Habit carves and molds character,
Which makes the big decisions.

What does that tell you? Even the little things count. If ever you're tempted to cut corners and do things the easy way, or do your work halfheartedly because others aren't watching, eventually your little choices are going to become habits that affect the bigger decisions you make in life. This is especially true with regard to sin. Taking it lightly can lead to poor decision-making down the road. So consider every choice carefully, no matter how small, for it will affect the bigger decisions you make.

God, help me to pay attention to my activities today and to consider the importance of the small choices I will make. May each one be a reflection of my one big choice to follow You. Amen.

Understanding Temptation

When it comes to *temptation* and *sin*, there's an important distinction to make: Temptation is not sin. When you are tempted, you are faced with a choice. You still have the opportunity to resist and not fall into sin. But when you succumb, then you've gone from temptation to sin.

So if you find yourself struggling with temptation, you haven't done anything wrong yet. Just make sure you look to God for help, for He has promised, "No temptation has overtaken you except such as is common to man; but God is faithful, who will not allow you to be tempted beyond what you are able, but with the temptation will also make the way of escape, that you may be able to bear it" (1 Corinthians 10:13).

Lord, thank You for the promise that You will help me to bear every temptation that comes my way today. When I am tempted, help me remember to run to You. Amen.

Winning
the Battle

When it comes to temptation, you are not alone. The Bible says this struggle is "common to man" (1 Corinthians 10:13). That means we all battle with temptation and sin. And thankfully, God has given you the resources you need for victory:

a new law (life in Christ),
a guide (the Holy Spirit),
a guidebook (the Bible),
and guides (wise counselors).

So you are fully equipped to withstand the temptations you face each day. Statements of "I can't" no longer apply to us. In Jesus Christ, it's "I can!" As Paul said, "I *can* do all things through Christ who strengthens me" (Philippians 4:13).

> *God, I affirm that You have given me everything I need to win the battle over temptation. When I am tempted, please help me remember to say, "In Christ, I can defeat this!" Amen.*

Protecting Yourself

God promised that when it comes to temptation, He has provided "the way of escape" (1 Corinthians 10:13). But even before you get to the point you are tempted, there are measures you can take to protect yourself from falling into sin.

First, you have God's Word, which helps you to discern right from wrong. Reading, listening to, and obeying it will help you resist sin. *Second*, you can avoid places and situations where you might experience temptation. *Third*, you can avoid getting involved with people who might pressure you to participate in sin. And fourth, avoid allowing your eyes to roam. Job "made a covenant with [his] eyes not to look lustfully at a young woman" (Job 31:1 NIV).

Providing temptation with fewer opportunities to strike is a great way to protect and preserve yourself.

Heavenly Father, lead me not into temptation today. And help me make smart choices about where I go, what I fill my mind with, and whom I spend my time with. Amen.

Your Weapon
Against Temptation

Have you ever noticed how Jesus handled temptation?

When Satan tempted the Lord during His 40 days in the wilderness, Jesus responded to every temptation by saying, "It is written...It is written...It is written" (Matthew 4:4-10). Why? Because God's Word is truth, and only truth can refute the lies Satan sends our way when he tempts us. Satan wants us to believe sin will give us pleasure and satisfaction. By contrast, God's truth warns that sin leads to guilt and emptiness.

Are you well-armed with God's Word? Do you know what it says? Are you fighting your battles against temptation with the sword of the Spirit, the Word of God (Ephesians 6:17)? Get to know what the Bible says about the kinds of temptations you face.

Lord, help me to identify the lies that are likely to bombard me today. Thank You for arming me with the truth and teaching me to use the sword of the Spirit effectively. Amen.

Leading by Serving

I'm sure you agree that Jesus Christ was the most influential man who ever lived. No one has or ever will match the impact He had.

What makes Him all the more remarkable is He wasn't an autocrat, a leader running roughshod over people or demanding respect and obedience. Rather, He was a humble servant. He "did not come to be served, but to serve, and to give His life" (Mark 10:45). After He performed the lowly task of washing the disciples' feet, He said, "I have given you an example, that you should do as I have done to you" (John 13:15).

Whose feet could you wash today? What opportunities do you have right now to serve rather than be served?

Jesus, You are the King of kings and Lord of lords, yet You chose to live as a humble servant. May I follow in Your steps today as You give me opportunities to serve those around me. Amen.

It Really
Does Matter

Sometimes we do an act of service and then get the feeling that it wasn't a valuable enough contribution to the church, or that nobody noticed or cared. Therefore we feel like what we did was a failure. It didn't really matter.

But no service that is done for God is a failure. Though from a human standpoint your labors might be overlooked or underappreciated, from a divine standpoint, that's never the case. God knows everything you do, and He will bless and reward you accordingly.

While recognition and thank-yous are nice to receive, they're not the reason you serve the Lord. You serve to please and honor Him. And the joy that comes from serving Him well will satisfy you more than any human applause could.

Father, thank You for seeing everything—even what is done in secret. As I find opportunities to serve others today, help me to remember that my reward comes from You. Amen.

Energized by Love

There is no greater example of loving service than that seen in a mother. It's remarkable the great sacrifice a mom makes for her children when they're feeling sick or they're struggling with something in their life.

Did you know the apostle Paul served with that kind of love? In his letter to the Christians in Thessalonica, he wrote, "We were gentle among you, just as a nursing mother cherishes her own children...we were well pleased to impart to you...our own lives, because you had become dear to us" (1 Thessalonians 2:7-8).

Is your service energized by love as well? Do you show love to those whom you serve?

Lord, I confess that my love is often shallow and weak. Please pour Your love into me and through me to touch everyone I meet today, especially those who feel rejected and alone. Amen.

What Service
Communicates

Do you realize that even if you say nothing to the people you serve, you are still teaching volumes? You nurture others by your Christlike example of selfless service. What wife wouldn't be built up and encouraged by a husband who loved her by helping make her job as a wife and mother easier? What child wouldn't be motivated and inspired to follow Christ after having seen the Lord's love demonstrated by his or her own father? What co-worker wouldn't see that there's something different about a Christian when you serve wholeheartedly without complaint?

Your nurturing service to others at home, at church, or on the job—providing help, encouragement, and hope—will point unbelievers toward God and edify believers in their faith.

Father, may my humble service to others today shout out the tremendously good news that You are reconciling us to Yourself and restoring us according to Your original design. Amen.

For the
Good of Others

By definition, serving others means being willing to make sacrifices for their good. A supreme example of this is the Good Samaritan in Luke 10:30-37. He sacrificed time by stopping to help the wounded traveler. He sacrificed his possessions by bandaging and dressing the man's wounds. He sacrificed his personal transportation by carrying the man to an inn. He sacrificed his life by taking care of the man personally. And he sacrificed his money by giving a day's wages and in essence a blank check to an innkeeper for the continued care of the wounded man.

Do you think the Good Samaritan had a positive impact? Without a doubt! When you serve, then, don't focus on what you've given up, but on what others have gained.

God, all I have is Yours. Help me to joyfully sacrifice my time and possessions for others today, mindful that You will supply all I need according to Your riches in glory in Christ Jesus. Amen.

A Heart
for Service

If your desire is for God to use you more as a servant, the most important first step you can take is to make sure you're serving those who live under your roof—your wife and children. What you are at home is what you are!

Then look at your major life commitments, such as your job. There, you'll find many opportunities to show Christlike love, sacrifice, and patience toward others. And if you belong to a club or sports team, showing a servant's heart in everything you do will cause people to see God and Christianity in a positive light.

The more you manifest a servant's heart in all you do, the more of an impact you'll have on people's lives.

> *Lord, open my eyes today so I can see opportunities to serve my family, my co-workers, and my friends. Help me to serve with joy as You strengthen me through Your Word and Spirit. Amen.*

Giving
Your All

When you serve, sometimes you can fall into the mind-set that because you're doing it for free, or because people should be grateful for your sacrifice, it's okay if you do less than your very best. You may rationalize that it's okay to cut corners.

But a good servant gives his all. For example, the apostle Paul told the Christian leaders in Ephesus, "Remember that for three years I did not cease to warn everyone night and day with tears" (Acts 20:31). He sacrificed himself without ceasing—and to the point of tears!

Do you view your opportunities to serve as a stewardship from God? When you do, you'll find yourself motivated to serve with excellence.

Father, help me to serve with excellence today, mindful that my service to others is pleasing to You. Thank You for Paul's inspiring example— may I follow in his steps. Amen.

When the Going
Gets Tough

A servant of God is willing to endure pain, suffering, and persecution in order to accomplish God's work. Remember the apostle Paul? He faced tremendous adversity—prisons, beatings, and even shipwreck. Yet his ministry bore much fruit—all because he was willing to keep going.

How firm are you in your commitment to serve? Do you give up easily at the least sign of resistance? Or are you willing to withstand the opposition that often arises in the course of serving the Lord?

When you find yourself getting discouraged, remember the examples of Paul and Jesus. They paid a great price, yet realized even greater gains. Hang in there, for what you do will reap eternal rewards.

> *God, thank You for strengthening me with all power according to Your glorious might so that I may have great endurance and patience. Because You are committed to me, I can be committed to You. Amen.*

A Life
Without Regrets

Paul saw his life as a sacrificial offering to God. He wrote, "I am already being poured out as a drink offering, and the time of my departure is at hand. I have fought the good fight, I have finished the race, I have kept the faith" (2 Timothy 4:6-7).

Because Paul had given his all, he could say he was ready to leave earth. He didn't have any regrets haunting him. With the Lord's help, he had done his job well, like a soldier who has completed his mission or a runner who has finished a race.

Are you living so that in the end you will have no regrets? Endeavor, by God's grace, to live each day to its fullest, and to give your all.

> *Lord, the race is long, but I am committed to running well as You fill me with strength. Empower me to live this very day in such a way that I will finish it with no regrets. Amen.*

The
Hidden You

The vast majority of an iceberg is hidden underwater. And what's true about icebergs is true about you. Your inner life, much like the mass of an iceberg, is hidden from the public eye. Yet the way you handle your secret life will have an impact on the part that people can see.

Which is why the Bible says, "Be sure your sin will find you out" (Numbers 32:23). And, "As [a man] thinks in his heart, so is he" (Proverbs 23:7). Whatever is true about your heart will eventually surface for all to see.

Only when your inner life is right will your outer life be right as well. Is there anything you need to bring to God today so the hidden part of you doesn't impair your outer influence?

> *Father, You are the only one who knows everything in my heart. Cleanse me, Lord, and heal me so that I can live with a whole heart and a pure and single focus. Amen.*

Cultivating Inner Purity

What are some practical ways you can keep your inner life pure?

- Develop firm convictions about doing what is right according to God's Word.
- Maintain a life of discipline that encourages holiness and avoids temptation.
- Make sure your goals are God-centered and not self-centered.
- Hide God's Word in your heart so it shapes your decisions and choices.
- Live a servant-oriented life focused on others rather than self.

Yielding your inner life to God in these ways will empower you to live the kind of outer life that honors the Lord and blesses others.

God, I want to live my life from the inside out today. May my convictions, personal discipline, and goals be up-to-date and shaped by Your Word. Help me to serve others with a pure heart. Amen.

Committing to Excellence

Legendary football coach Vince Lombardi said, "The quality of your life will be determined by the depth of your commitment to excellence, no matter what your chosen field." With that in mind, here are some questions you can ask yourself:

- What are the most important commitments in my life?
- Can I honestly say I'm giving my best to those commitments?
- How can I do better at carrying out those commitments, and what price am I willing to pay to make that happen?

Those questions will help you evaluate your priorities, and your answers will enable you to determine how to best spend your time and energy.

Lord, help me to be honest today as I assess what I'm actually committed to. Do I need to reprioritize my commitments? What steps do I need to take to follow through? Lead me, Lord. Amen.

Going Beyond
What Is Expected

To excel at something is to go over and above the normal. It means doing more than what is expected. It's about taking the extra step, the extra time, the extra effort in whatever you do. Yes, it's hard work, but in the end, if you persevere, it'll pay off.

Taking extra time with your wife and children will result in closer, stronger relationships with them. Going the extra mile on the job will gain appreciation from your boss and co-workers. Giving that extra effort as you serve in your church or help someone in need will bring blessing to others.

Without question, it pays to give your very best. Won't you ask the Lord to strengthen your resolve to strive for excellence in all that you do?

> *Father, show me today where I have been cutting corners. Empower me through Your Word and Spirit to go beyond what is expected and to demonstrate Your amazing love. Amen.*

Imparting
Your Life

One reason the apostle Paul's ministry still affects us today is that he was thoroughly focused on pouring his life into other people. To the church leaders in Ephesus he said, "I kept back nothing that was helpful" (Acts 20:20), and he did this for three years (verse 31). To the Christians in Thessalonica he said, "We were well pleased to impart to you...our own lives" (1 Thessalonians 2:8). And he worked with Timothy for 15 years, equipping him to carry the baton of leadership.

The famous preacher John Wesley said, "God buries his workmen, but His work goes on." Are you that kind of workman? Are you pouring yourself into others, including your children? If so, your impact will continue long after you're gone.

God, help me to honestly assess my impact on others. Whom should I pour my life into? How should I do that? May I influence others for good through the power of Your Spirit. Amen.

A Pattern
to Follow

Jesus was the greatest mentor of all time. He took a ragtag group of uneducated, ill-equipped men and, in three years, molded them into a force that turned the world upside down. Here's what we can learn from His example:

There can be no impact without contact. Jesus spent time with His men. He taught by word and example, cared for them, and was patient with them.

He looked for men who were willing to learn. When He called them to the ministry, they eagerly followed. They made mistakes, but were willing to listen and obey.

He expected His disciples to make disciples. Jesus commanded them to carry on His work. We're now a part of that work, and we're to pass it on to others.

> *Lord, empower me today to follow Your example. Help me to pay attention to others, to learn from them, and to offer my input when they are willing to receive it. Amen.*

Assessing Your Impact

The closer you get to another person, the more influence you will have on that person's life.

And that brings up some important questions: Who are you getting close to? Who are you pouring your life into? Will you one day be able to join the apostle Paul in saying, "I have fought the good fight, I have finished the race" (2 Timothy 4:7) because you have equipped others to excel in following the Lord and serving Him?

Remember that it's not numbers or stature that's important here. Influencing your children and those closest to you takes priority over those outside your home. And it's far better to influence a few people well than many people poorly. Adhering to these principles will help you to finish the race well.

Father, does my family feel close to me? Whom am I influencing for good? Help me to be a good steward of the relationships You have given me. Amen.

Your Legacy

What will you leave behind when you are gone? As you well know, only that which is spiritual will last. If all you leave behind are personal memories, they will fade with time. If you leave financial security and provisions, that will take care of people's temporary physical needs, but nothing more.

By contrast, if you leave a godly example and you've helped people grow more spiritually strong, you'll have given gifts that last for eternity. You'll have left treasures that can be passed on to future generations of believers. That, in a very real way, is what it means to "lay up for yourselves treasures in heaven" rather than on earth (Matthew 6:19-20).

God, how is my heavenly treasure account doing? Show me today some simple ways that I can make a lasting impression on others and help them follow You. Amen.

Men
Growing Men

You are most likely very grateful for those spiritually mature men who have taken the time to help you grow as a Christian. Likewise, everything you do for the next generation of Christian men will elicit their gratitude as well.

When it comes to choosing the right men to pour your life into, what should you look for?

- Look for *faithful* men. Find men who are trustworthy, who keep their word.
- Look for *available* men. Find men who are willing to sacrifice their time for ministry training.
- Look for *teachable* men. Find men who are eager to learn. Their hunger will ensure your time and energy are well-spent.

Lord, the thought of pouring my life into younger Christians is a bit intimidating. Open the doors, I pray, and help me to simply share with others the things You have taught me. Amen.

A Living Bible

Have you ever considered that for some people in your life, you might be the only Christian they know? They may see believers on TV or in the newspaper, but often those portrayals are in a negative light. You may be the only one they can interact with in person. It's been said in a poem that "you are a living Bible, known and read by men." The rhyme goes on to ask, "What does the Bible say, 'according to you'?"

So are you exhibiting a proper representation of Christianity? Are you kind, thoughtful, and approachable? What would people say about God based on what they see of your life? What does the Bible say, according to you?

Father, this sounds like such a responsibility! Are You sure You want me to be Your representative? But I'm willing, Lord—please speak to others through my words and actions. Amen.

Well Done!

There is coming a day when your time on earth will end. But hopefully that won't be true about your influence as a man after God's own heart. No, as you are faithful to pour your life into your family, your friends, your workmates, and fellow believers at church, your influence will live on in their lives. You'll be gone, but God's work done through you will continue. You, as His messenger, will no longer speak, but God's message will live on.

May you never lose sight of the calling to live as a man after God's own heart. For in the end, you'll get the greatest reward anyone could ever hope to receive—that of hearing the Lord Jesus Christ say to you, "Well done, good and faithful servant."

> *God, I don't know how many decades I will have to serve You, but I do know I have today. When this very day ends, may I sense You whispering, "Well done." Amen.*

Other Books by Jim George

The Bare Bones Bible® Handbook
The perfect resource for a fast and friendly overview of every book of the Bible. Includes the grand theme and main points of each book, the key men and women of God and what you can learn from them, the major events in Bible history, and personal applications for spiritual growth and daily living.

The Bare Bones Bible® Handbook for Teens
Based on the bestselling *Bare Bones Bible® Handbook,* this edition includes content and life applications specially written with teens in mind! They will be amazed at how much the Bible has to say about the things that matter most to them—their happiness, friends and family, home and school, and goals for the future. Great for youth group studies!

The Bare Bones Bible® Facts
This book brings Bible facts to life through more than 150 carefully selected topics that provide fascinating insights about important historical events, interesting customs and cultural practices, and significant people and places.

10 Minutes to Knowing the Men and Women of the Bible
The lessons you can learn from the outstanding men and women of the Bible are powerfully relevant for today. As you review their lives through the biographical sketches in this book, you'll discover special qualities worth emulating and life lessons for everyday living, which will energize your spiritual growth.

A Leader After God's Own Heart

What makes a man a truly good leader—one God can use? Jim George looks at 15 ways to lead with strength, and to have a positive and lasting impact on others.

A Man After God's Own Heart

Many Christian men want to be men after God's own heart… but how do they do this? George shows that a heartfelt desire to practice God's priorities is all that's needed. God's grace does the rest. Includes study guide. This book has appeared on the Evangelical Christian Booksellers Association's bestseller list.

A Husband After God's Own Heart

Husbands will find their marriages growing richer and deeper as they pursue God and discover 12 areas in which they can make a real difference in their relationship with their wife. (This book was a 2005 Gold Medallion Award Finalist.)

The Man Who Makes a Difference

What made the apostle Paul so effective, so influential? Readers will experience true fulfillment as they learn how they can make a real and lasting difference in the workplace, at home, at church, and in their community.

A Young Man After God's Own Heart

Pursuing God really *is* an adventure—a lot like climbing a mountain. There are all kinds of challenges on the way up, but the awesome view at the top is well worth the trip. This book helps teen men to experience the thrill of knowing real success in life—the kind that counts with God. (This book was a 2006 Gold Medallion Award Finalist.)

A Young Man's Guide to Making Right Choices

This book will help teen men to think carefully about their decisions, assuring a more fulfilling and successful life. A great resource for gaining the skills needed to face life's challenges.

The Remarkable Prayers of the Bible

Jim looks deeply into prayers of great men and women in the Bible and shares more than a hundred practical applications that can help shape your life and prayers. A separate *Growth and Study Guide* is also available.

A Little Boy After God's Own Heart

(*coauthored with Elizabeth George*)

With delightful artwork by Judy Luenebrink, this book encourages young boys in the virtues of patience, goodness, faithfulness, sharing, and more. Written to help boys discover how special they are, these rhymes present wisdom and character traits for life.

God Loves His Precious Children

(*coauthored with Elizabeth George*)

Jim and Elizabeth George share the comfort and assurance of Psalm 23 with young children. Engaging watercolor scenes and delightful rhymes bring the truths and promises of each verse to life.

God's Wisdom for Little Boys

(*coauthored with Elizabeth George*)

The wonderful teachings of Proverbs come to life for boys. Memorable rhymes play alongside colorful paintings for an exciting presentation of truths to live by.

ABOUT THE AUTHOR

Jim George is a teacher and speaker and an award-winning, bestselling author of numerous books, including *A Man After God's Own Heart* and *The Bare Bones Bible*® *Handbook*. To order any of his books, email Jim at:

www.JimGeorge.com

Jim and Elizabeth George Ministries
P.O. Box 2879
Belfair, WA 98528
1-800-542-4611